Rubber Suits & Lukewarm Soup
Surviving Life as an Oceanic Ferry Pilot

First Edition: Self-Published May 2017 (American English Edition)
ISBN 978-1-387-02479-7

Printed in the United States of America
To order additional copies of this book: www.redwoodbusdriver.com or www.lulu.com ID: 20935523

Front Cover Photo: An Atlantic Ocean sunset from a Cirrus SR22
Back Cover Photo: Approaching Windhoek Airport in Namibia, Africa

Rubber Suits & Lukewarm Soup

Surviving Life as an Oceanic Ferry Pilot

By Steve Randall

For Andrea and my family

**Dedicated to the memory of those
ferry pilots who did not survive.**

Jim Beaton, Greg Frey, Jeff Hall, Hardy Kalitzki,
Lori Love, Alexandra Kuipers, Don Ratliff,
Fritz Schröder, Kelvin Stark and 'Greenland' Simon.

**Thank you for guiding, coaching and
encouraging me through my journey.**

Larry Bax, David Curties, Louisa Dickson,
John Gijsen, Pam Heather, Rob Hirst, Les Hounsome,
Peter Hunter, Robin Musham, Rob Oade,
Tony Sheppard and Joe Thorne.

Contents

Introduction

"I don't need to pick up pennies,
I've already had my fair share of good luck."

THE MILKY WAY is clearly visible cutting through a blanket of stars tonight. It is a gorgeous evening to be flying. The volcanic peaks of Maui are two hours behind us and we are in smooth air, level at 37,000 feet. My 149 passengers are comfortable and many are sleeping as we speed across the Pacific towards a morning sunrise in San Francisco. Our next reporting point is twenty minutes ahead of us, all systems are operating normally and we are on-time. I recline my seat a little, take a sip of coffee and dim the cockpit lights. Immediately, my office window is filled with a million intricate light patterns from a night sky unpolluted by the yellow glare of civilization. Several constellations are easy to pick out but I continue to scan the sky for the chance of glimpsing a star that nobody has seen before. It is a breathtaking and privileged view I have enjoyed countless times before, but not always from the comfort of a modern jet airliner cockpit.

My path to command this commercial jet included several years as an international aircraft delivery pilot, an extremely dangerous occupation more commonly called "ferry flying." For several years, I specialized in the delivery of very small, sparsely equipped training aircraft, flying thousands of miles across our oceans to owners and brokers throughout the world. I often flew alone surrounded by huge temporary fuel tanks installed where the passenger seats would normally be, in aircraft no larger than a family car with four seats and a propeller at the front driven by a single piston engine. Most of these machines were barely capable of scraping over an average sized mountain and many lacked basic equipment, like an autopilot or satellite navigation, for ferry flights that could last up to 18 hours. None of the smaller aircraft I flew were designed to confront the types of extreme and unpredictable weather systems that occasionally build in the North Atlantic or Pacific Ocean and so a thorough understanding of low level oceanic weather systems was a mandatory skill I had to learn as I traveled.

Although my ferry pilot career was initially accidental, I worked hard to build my reputation as a reliable and safe delivery pilot. My first few solo oceanic crossings were extremely risky and blind luck was an overwhelming substitute for inexperience. The small group of professional oceanic ferry pilots designated me "the new English guy" while I earned my experience. Shaking this title took almost a full year of back-to-back oceanic ferrying before I was confident I had witnessed and survived most of the hazardous weather conditions that exist across our oceans. Once my rookie season was completed, I'd watch other new pilots go through the same period of self-education, but the turnover rate was extremely high. Many green pilots would simply quit part way through a delivery, usually after they had witnessed some of the true dangers. Tragically, and all too often, some would never reach their destination. Occasionally, very seasoned ferry pilots would get into trouble too. Good ferry pilots like Hardy, Alexandra, Simon, Jeff, Lori, Jim, Don and Fritz are all dead. It would have been easy for me to join them if my handful of luck hadn't kept me safe while I continuously crisscrossed the earth.

Hearing of a ferry pilot loss, rookie or experienced, always hit me extremely hard. I would often think about my missing colleagues as I flew low across the sea, following the same routes they had once flown. Sickening loneliness would often commandeer my mind as I approached the middle of the ocean, especially when I was too far away from civilization for any "post ditching" rescue. It was at these times that I'd turn to the stars for distraction. I tried to learn new constellations and I slowly mapped the night sky in my head during hours of unaccompanied study time. As my engine droned on towards another landing, I would attempt to turn my thoughts to the enthusiastic people waiting for my arrival. Most aircraft owners were barely able to control their excitement as I touched-down after a flight from a journey originating on the other side of the world. I could always pick out a beaming smile as I taxied in and it was a privilege to hand over the keys at the end of a successful delivery flight. The satisfaction of completing each delivery was one of the thrills that kept me going, despite the dangers.

Becoming a ferry pilot was an unlikely mix of circumstance, bureaucracy, error, determination and stubbornness. It is not a journey I'd recommend to anyone but the interesting people I met, the varied aircraft I flew, the cultures I witnessed, the weather I fought and the close calls I experienced as I flew over our borderless earth inspired me to write some of my stories down. Recalling every detail has been tricky and I relied on logbooks and some old navigation logs to trigger enough material to keep the stories somewhat interesting. It is inevitable that I have mixed up some of the events during this process and so mistakes and omissions are mine alone. Most of my ferry flights were long, boring and relatively uneventful and so I have merged fragments of other unrelated ferry flights into many of my stories. I have removed or altered names, events, aircraft and places where I felt it necessary or where my memory has failed me.

I am a pilot, not a writer but every pilot has a story to tell. This is my story of surviving life as an oceanic ferry pilot. They are memories I will cherish forever and I hope you enjoy them too.

Steve Randall, August 2017

Another Atlantic Ocean crossing in my rubber suit.

PART ONE

DAYDREAM

Delivery Route

"So, you want to fly for a living?
Consider a cocaine habit instead;
it will be cheaper and much less addictive."

SINKING

I AM NINETEEN years old, standing alone and naked in the tiny kitchen of a small room I am renting. A dirty plate from my last meal is in the sink, so I move it and climb into the cold aluminum basin. It's a tight fit and I barely have enough room to maneuver. I attach a small length of hosepipe to the faucet and turn on the water to begin my morning shower. I pay little attention to the sound of the mice scurrying around behind the kitchen wall as I lather up some soap to use as shampoo. As I finish, I hear the rain begin to hit the window across the room. I sigh at the depressingly familiar routine. It's going to be another cold and miserable English day.

My room is on the second floor of an old Victorian student house in the south of England. Not much light makes it through the window and the single light bulb does little to illuminate the dark corners. Patches of green mold grow where the wall and ceiling meet. There are four other tenants in the house and we share a communal shower. The landlord knows that we all have money troubles but this hasn't stopped him from installing a meter to the shower unit. A three-minute shower costs forty pence, which is less that the cost of a Snickers bar, but I am in a circle of debt and I simply can't afford to feed the meter every day. Luckily, I found the piece of hosepipe in the front yard a few weeks back and I immediately knew how I could use it to save myself some money. My landlord cannot charge me for the hot water that comes to my little kitchen sink and so I attach the hosepipe every morning and shower using gallons and gallons of steaming hot, and FREE, water!

I'd be happy to pay for a shower every few days but I recently got a job to try and help myself out of debt and so I need to look and smell the part. Ironically, I am a personal loans officer for a small finance company. The owners are corrupt; I know one is heading to prison soon. I am encouraged to sell high interest loans to people who are in financial hardship, just like me. My customers have poor credit but we will happily loan money to them at an exorbitant interest rate. The rate is so high that almost all the monthly payment goes towards paying the interest, barely reducing the original debt. As expected, and as planned by the owners, many customers default on their payments and when they fail to pay I am directed to offer a consolidation plan, adding even more debt to the existing loan. Eventually, my unfortunate clients find themselves paying virtually every penny they earn to our greedy owners, who then spend the weekends converting the cash into champagne parties on board their speedboats. I hate this job but I need it if I have any chance of pursuing my true dream.

Few of my customers realize that I am in a similar financial position to them. I empathize with many and I quietly try to persuade some to talk to bankruptcy experts instead of entering the destructive cycle of consolidation financing. I set a poor example as I too have an outstanding loan with our company to pay for the car I need to travel to work. It is not exactly a luxury car but my eighteen-year-old rusty Mazda 323, with three different color doors and a silver stencil of a Christmas tree painted on the hood runs quite well. My boss "generously" cut the interest rate for my loan to the lowest our company offers, a rate still higher than most credit cards on the market, but my poor credit gives me few options. Once my monthly payment has been taken from my pitiful salary, I have just enough left to run the car and pay my room rent. Finding money for basics like food, clothes and hot showers is a balancing act I face each month.

The meter on the shower is one of several in the house. Another small gray box sits in the corner of my room; this one is for the electricity. The landlord has set the meter rate very high and I simply don't have enough money to keep feeding it. Winter is coming and it is bitterly cold during the evenings. I try to save electricity by laying under my heavy blanket with the lights out while I listen to the couple downstairs argue or screw for my entertainment. I really need a little more electricity so I can heat my room; without it, I simply can't stay warm or dry my clothes. I try to drip-dry my shirts over the kitchen sink but the cold air in the room keeps them damp. In the past, I used an iron to dry my shirts but the dials on the electricity meter spin out of control when I do this, and the faster the dials spin the closer I am to having no more electricity.

The meter consumes much of my attention as I never seem to have enough coins to feed it. I sit and curse the stupid box, waiting for the familiar loud click as the money runs out and the electricity is cut off. If the landlord would set the meter to a reasonable rate I could probably manage my electricity use, but he's scamming us just as he is with the shower meter. Enough is enough. I decide to find out how this contraption works and so I head to the local library and read *The Complete Guide to Wiring*. With my new-found knowledge, I grab a blunt dinner knife from the kitchen drawer and begin to carefully and systematically dismantle the ugly metal box. I study the wires hidden behind the contraption and soon discover how to re-wire them, bypassing the meter. It works! At last, I have unlimited electricity and I am overjoyed with my work. I have light in the evening, I have music and I acquire a small abandoned oil heater for my room.

There is one problem looming on the horizon. At the end of each month, the landlord comes by to empty the meters in the house. His next visit is in two weeks and I know that there will be too few coins sitting in the locked metal box. Somehow, I need to find a way to put a few more coins in to try and keep him off the scent. I devise a plan. First, I cut my food spending by buying a bag of potatoes from a local store. These are old potatoes, many with stalks growing from them, so I negotiate a 50% discount for the bag. Chipped, baked, fried and mashed - every night is potato night! Next, I study a road map and find two new routes to get to and from work. The routes are shorter with a few downhill segments allowing me to coast and save some fuel. I over-inflate my tires a little to help further reduce my gas mileage and to stretch every drop of fuel I can. Next, I get a newspaper route. It doesn't pay much but it forces me out of the lonely room and every penny I earn will go towards masking my inflated use of electricity. I may be the oldest paper boy in town and I've been chased by every dog in the neighborhood but having heat and light in my room is worth it.

The landlord is coming to empty the electricity meter tomorrow. I have fifteen one-pound coins to show for my efforts of the past couple of weeks. I am desperate to spend the money on food but I know that my landlord expects to see triple the number of coins that I currently have in my hand. My plan is on track but I still have some work to do before he arrives in the morning. I begin by making the room look a little more disheveled than normal. I hide the heater, radio and iron at the back of a closet and cover them with some bed sheets. I find temporary hiding places for several of my meager belongings until the room looks completely bare and empty. I spread out some of the sparse furniture to add to the authenticity of emptiness and throw as many blankets as I can on top of the bed to demonstrate how I keep warm without electricity. I hang some damp clothes on hangers over the sink and open a window to ensure that the room will be suitably cold by the morning. I almost forget to hide my "shower" hosepipe under the mattress. Before I sleep, I feed my precious coins into the meter and put it back to its original state trying hard not to electrocute myself or set fire to the house. I am pleased with my work but tomorrow will prove whether my efforts have been worthwhile.

I am shivering as I awake in my tiny freezing room early the next morning. The stage is set and I am ready to execute the final part of my plan and convince the skinflint landlord that I am the most frugal tenant he has ever encountered. There is a knock on my door; it's my landlord. Adrenaline is racing through me but I scruff up my hair a little and take a moment to compose myself. He comes into the room and goes straight to the meter. I think he has noticed a small piece of plaster that has fallen from the wall beneath the gray box. I probably knocked it with the knife last night. He seems suspicious but I say nothing as he empties out my hard-earned coins, too few for his liking. He doesn't seem to believe that I have used such a small amount of electricity. He stares at me, locking eyes and looking for answers but I've rehearsed my story and my answers are polished and convincing. He looks around the cold room and sees the wet clothes dripping into the sink. As an unplanned bonus, the mice begin running through the walls, helping to validate my desperate tale. He leaves, mumbling something about increasing the electricity rates. I peek from my window to confirm that he has left. As I see his car disappear up the road I jump around the room ecstatic with my performance. I fist pump the air as I retrieve my heater and immediately set to work on the meter re-wire. I gather my hidden belongings, singing *We are the champions* to myself. It is when I hold the small shower hose that my mood suddenly changes and I stop singing.

It hits me like a ton of bricks. This really is my life. An endless circle of poverty and debt in a lonely damp room that I share with a family of mice. The picture I created for my landlord is a hairs width from reality. When I left school, I was convinced that I'd become a pilot; it's all I ever wanted to do with my life. I spent countless hours studying aviation books and skipped many days of "useless" mandatory education to hang out at the airport in the belief that I was learning my trade. But all I can do now is look out of my window and up at the overcast sky. I want to fly so desperately but as I catch my reflection in the window I see a harsh reality looking back at me. My silly dream will forever be out of my reach. I feel absolutely deflated as I undress and re-attach the hose to the faucet. I ease myself into the sink as the rain begins to hit the window. I am already late for work and I need to shower.

SMOOTH, SMOOTH, SMOOTH

It is six years earlier and I recently turned thirteen years old. Aircraft fascinate both my dad and me. A new aviation museum has just opened in our hometown of Southampton and we are visiting it for the first time today. Just walking into the large hall full of shiny aircraft takes my breath away. There are helicopters, gliders, several old jets and some gleaming wartime fighters squeezed into the tall building. A huge four-engine passenger flying boat takes center stage, a Shorts Sandringham. It is an incredible sight and we head straight for the line to get a cockpit tour. I barely pay attention to the elaborate interior of the old aircraft as I am keen to get into the cockpit. A young boy, not much older than me, is conducting the tour today. This really surprises me but he seems very knowledgeable. He is wearing a smart blue uniform and I catch a glimpse of the badge on his arm, *Air Training Corps*.

The cockpit of the flying boat is a magnificent sight. There is a bank of dials for the engineer, a desk with charts for the navigator and various knobs and switches for the radio operator. As fascinating as these areas are, I am instinctively drawn forward towards the pilot's seat. I sit in the captain's chair on the left side. I am captivated by the view and my senses are completely overwhelmed. I could sit here all day holding the large control wheel and breathing in the smell of old oil and leather. My hand reaches down and follows the contour of the four tall throttle levers in the center panel. It all feels so wonderful and very natural. Never have I been so sure that something felt so right and I have a strong sense that I belong in this seat.

As we continue to walk around the museum, I begin to think about whether I could become a pilot. I desperately need a direction to understand if I could achieve my new goal and a thousand questions come into my head. "Why should I waste time studying school topics not related to flying and end up sitting behind a boring desk in a dull office?" I look back up at the cockpit of the flying boat. That's the office I want and those are the office windows I want to look through. My future is becoming so clear to me but it seems impossibly far away. Where do I even start? Then, I have an idea; what if I could give the cockpit tour? If I could learn how to give cockpit tours of the flying boat, just like that boy, then I would have a chance to learn what every instrument does and how this enormous aircraft once flew.

My mind is spinning with possibilities until my dad and I stop next to an incredible machine that leaves me speechless. It's a Supermarine Spitfire, with a beautiful elliptical wing and stunning flowing lines. It was originally designed and built in Southampton, just a "stones throw" from where we are standing. The prototype, K5054, first flew in 1936 at our local airport in Eastleigh. My mind stops all thoughts for a moment and I stare at every perfect rivet and the immaculate panel work of the fuselage and wings. Behind me, a door opens with a bang and I look over. There are dozens of boys wearing the *Air Training Corps* uniform. I can see into a large room behind the door, filled with large flight simulators and long tables with maps spread out on them. I inch towards the door to get a better look but the door closes again. I decide to begin my journey by finding out more about the *Air Training Corps*, how I can join, how

I can fly those simulators and how I can give cockpit tours of the flying boat.

It is a month later and I am the newest junior cadet with the *Air Training Corps*. I will spend two evenings each week learning aircraft recognition, learning to target shoot, learning basic survival and learning to conduct tours on the museum flying boat. I am already having a blast with my likeminded fellow squadron friends. We talk about aviation almost non-stop. A note posted on the squadron wall catches my eye: "Sign up here for Air Experience Flights."

It is the morning of 14th June 1986 and I am debating whether to have breakfast. I am with ten other cadets at Hurn Airport in the south of England. We are all around the same age of 14. Today is the day of our first flight experience with the Royal Air Force. Our bus has arrived at the airport too early and so we are having breakfast at the terminal. I won't admit it but my stomach is turning with a mix of excitement and fear. As I look at the fried eggs and bacon in front of me, I wonder if they will soon fill an embarrassing sick bag during my flight. It will be hard to hide this from my friends after landing. One of the cadets asks an instructor about being airsick. The chatter lowers as we all listen to the answer, each pretending not to be too concerned about the prospect. One of the officers says that we should eat heartily. "It's far more comfortable to throw something up than nothing at all," he says. I look around at my fellow cadets. We are struggling with the advice, wondering if it's a test. I decide to eat the eggs and leave the bacon.

It is a short bus journey to the other side of the airport. I stare through the bus window as we turn a corner and I get my first glimpse of the DeHavilland Chipmunk we will be flying in. This is the current Royal Air Force basic trainer, built in the 1950s, with a small wheel at the back and two main wheels at the front beneath the single propeller. There are four of these gleaming red and white aircraft sitting in the sun as we pull up. I can't take my eyes away from the wonderful machines as we walk past them to a small wooden building next to a large hangar. The sky is clear and blue; nothing will stop us from flying today. The fear is still present but the excitement is beginning to suppress it. We are all sitting in a large common room facing a white screen. The lights are turned off and a projector begins to show a safety video. I absorb everything and even the background music to the short movie gives me shivers. We watch closely as several safety items are explained: how to put the parachute on, how to tighten the strap on the "bone dome" helmet and how to safely get into the rear cockpit behind the pilot. Then the narrator says, "in the event of an emergency in flight the pilot will ask you to abandon the aircraft, simply slide back the canopy, stand up in your seat and dive toward the rear edge of the wing." I never considered jumping out of the Chipmunk before and the thought begins to play on my mind. "Pull the parachute handle, land with knees together and we will come and pick you up." The silence in the room mirrors the rising uneasiness as thoughts of parachuting into the cool English air are considered.

Soon enough, the film ends and we find our names on a list posted on the back wall. I will be the third to fly. I am glad not to be the first and I watch as the first two cadets nervously strap themselves into their parachutes. There is very little talk as we all watch. It's impossible for either cadet to stand fully upright once the straps are tightened, but they are soon guided out towards the small low wing planes, with propellers already turning. The first one takes off. I watch for wing movements and to see how quickly it is climbing. It seems like just a few minutes have passed, but I hear "Cadet Randall, it's your turn."

My hands are shaking a little as I feed the parachute strap through the metal loop, just as I remember seeing in the short movie. I'm not sure if it's nerves or excitement but I feel a little sick. I wish I hadn't had those eggs. Just like the first two cadets, I cannot stand fully upright because of the parachute straps. The actual parachute bag is hanging down behind me below my waist. It will become my seat when I get to take my place behind the pilot. I have a smelly rubber headset on underneath the helmet. I am also wearing a green lifejacket that sticks out from my chest. They call it a "Mae West," named after the wartime sex symbol who shares this chest protrusion!

I am being led towards a Chipmunk with the engine already running and the pilot in his seat up front. I notice the markings on the side, **WD373**. I remember the instructions from the film. I carefully keep my feet on the black rubber strips on the inside of the wing and pull myself up into the small cockpit. I sit on the parachute and it's quite comfortable. The aide clicks in the seat belts and plugs me into the communication cord. He closes the canopy and I look around. The smell is unusual but memorable; oil, fuel, old leather, and a lot of cadet sweat. A small control stick is in front of me just below the instrument panel. There are a few levers on the left side and a big lever on the right. I make a point to keep my hands away from them. "Hello, are you ready?" The radio is crackly. "Yes sir," I answer back. There is no going back now. I see a sick bag tucked into the panel ahead. I'll do anything not to use it. I see the stick come back and the power comes on. We are heading out to the runway. I breathe hard into the microphone. "Relax, you'll enjoy this," the pilot says.

It is 10:05am and the sun is shining through the canopy. The pilot opens the throttle fully and we start to charge down the runway. This is it. It's everything I have been thinking about for the past few weeks. I see the stick go forward to raise the tailwheel, then slightly backwards and we are in the air. I cannot stop smiling and I try to control my giggling so that the pilot doesn't hear. I feel every small bump at first, but it soon starts to feel like riding in a car on a slightly bumpy road. I really can't believe that I am finally in the air. The sensation is absolutely amazing! We zoom around some white cotton clouds, chopping up bits of them. This is a feeling I have never felt before; it is so wonderful. Soon enough, the instruction comes for me to hold the stick. "You have control," comes the order through my headset. "I have control Sir." As if to make the point that I am flying, I see the pilot raise his hands in the air. I am really flying this Chipmunk, oh my God. But, I cannot seem to keep it straight. Every movement I make seems jerky. I grab the stick with both hands but it's even worse than before. Perhaps I'm not meant to fly? Perhaps we are out of control? The pilot starts talking to me through the intercom. "If you have white knuckles right now, relax your grip, this is not a rollercoaster. One hand only. Smooth, smooth, smooth." The change is immediate. "There you go, you've got it." When I relax my grip the little plane goes where I want it to go. It was my shaking hands making all those jerky movements. I must relax. I take a deep breath. I try a little turn to the left and then right. I really CAN do this. "I have control," the pilot says after a few minutes. I am disappointed to be heading back so soon but I spend the next few minutes soaking up everything this beautiful machine is offering. I want to remember every detail that I can. We gently touch down on the wide runway. It is 10:35am and my life has changed forever. I am absolutely determined to fly for a living. Nothing will stop me. I want to be a professional pilot above all else.

We come to a stop. "Well done," says the voice from the front. I can see the next cadet waiting to replace me, hunched over with his mountain of equipment strapped on. The engine continues to turn and the canopy is slid back. I release the seat belts and stand up on the metal seat into the airflow. My feet find the rubber wing strips and I walk backwards down towards the ground. The pilot turns around to look at me. This is the first time I have seen his face. He smiles with a thumb up, which I eagerly return.

During the next year, I fly four more times in the Chipmunk. Two flights are basic aerobatic lessons and one introduces landings. I log 2 hours and 15 minutes of flying time into my new logbook. Joining the *Air Training Corps* was a great decision. I give tours of the flying boat cockpit on weekends and I rise to the rank of Flight Sergeant. I soon become an instructor with the simulator department, teaching basic instrument flying to cadets in small moveable Link trainers, which were originally used during the Second World War. I study every book and flight manual on the shelves of the simulator room and soon I teach on our DeHavilland Comet 4B simulator, a four-engine jet from the 1950s that was a variant of the world's first commercial jet airliner. I am in love with everything aviation.

I know I want to fly, but how can I afford it? The Queen has paid for my limited flying training so far and I am grateful, but if I fund my own flying training, a one-hour lesson costs well over one hundred pounds. I need a minimum of forty hours to get my basic flying license and I'd be lucky to receive one hundred pounds as a birthday gift. I can't wait forty years to get my license! There is simply no way that my working-class parents can afford to pay for my flying training. They live paycheck to paycheck, simply to cover the cost of our rent and food. They both work hard but never seem to have too much left over for themselves. We have pennies in our family and I need pounds, lots of them. Joining the Royal Air Force as a pilot seems like an obvious route. Fast jet is my preference but I'd be happy flying a Chipmunk all day long if that was available. I meet with an RAF careers advisor. I walk into the office with a smile on my face and enthusiasm running through my veins. "So, you wear glasses," he says. The comment throws me a little and the next news I receive is absolutely devastating. I can't believe it; my uncorrected eyesight is just below the entry standard required. He talks about other positions in the RAF but I am not interested. That is the end of the interview. I will never be allowed to fly in the military. In just a few minutes, my world has changed once again.

As I get up to leave, the recruiter mentions that my eyesight might be acceptable for civilian flying. It is as much incentive as I need to keep pursuing my dream. I'll go the civilian route and just figure out how to pay for it later. I leave the RAF office with an overwhelming desire to be an airline pilot.

REPO MAN

It is three years after my first Chipmunk flight and I realize I have hit this at completely the wrong time. None of the airlines are offering cadet classes or sponsorship. If I am going to fly I need money, but the sums involved run into tens of thousands of pounds. Along with the flying training I must also go to aviation school and pass the required twelve airline transport pilot exams. I see many loans in my future but I have nothing to secure them with and my bank account is empty. I am currently working part-time as a paint mixer and shelf-stacker at a hardware store, a job that will not impress a potential lender. Assuming I can figure out the money, should I start the flying first or start studying for the exams? How can I fit all of this in and continue with my "A" level college courses? I am told that I need qualifications to be competitive with other candidates and so I am studying mathematics and English literature. However, Shakespeare seems to have very little relevance to my aviation future and so I am completely bored with the schoolwork. None of the material is staying in my brain. I am very confused and I ache for some more direction.

I am out with my dad today. To make some extra money, he does a little commercial photography. He has a real talent for it but there is very little work to be found. We have driven thirty miles north of Southampton to a kitchen showroom. We meet the owner, an older gentleman with a white beard. He wants a few photos of his kitchen displays for an upcoming leaflet campaign. I help with the lighting and lenses. After an hour, we are done and we follow the

25

owner into his office to finish up. Something on his office wall catches my eye and I look twice before it registers. There is a photo of this man in an airline captain's uniform standing next to an old airliner. "Yes, that's me," he says. Following a downturn in the airline industry he decided to quit and open this showroom. He didn't recommend I go to the airlines. "It's a hard business to get into and airlines fail every year," he cautioned. This didn't matter to me.

He listens to my story, not saying too much. He knows that I won't be happy unless I try to fulfill my dream. He pauses before giving me his advice. "The airlines are not hiring right now so go and get a job, get a pilot's license and approach the airlines already qualified. Just enjoy getting your pilot's license and decide whether to continue after you get it." He completes his advice with, "study for the airline exams in the evenings, but be prepared for a great deal of work. If you can pass the exams, you will have a good shot at being an airline pilot." The weight of the world has been lifted from my shoulders, and all because of a silly kitchen appliance leaflet! This is a fantastic day. I am refocused and I'm determined to make this work without delay. I quit my irrelevant college course and sign up for aviation ground school classes instead. I must find a job and start to earn some good money. I see an employment posting. After a short interview, I accept a job at the finance company, move into the student room with the mice and buy the old multi-colored Mazda.

It is now two years later and the landlord has just left with the electricity meter money after another poverty performance and re-wire. Something has gone terribly wrong with my career plan. When I first took the finance company job, I did so to earn enough money to fly. But since then, I've done nothing but starve and pay bills. I can't even afford a train ticket to get to the airport, let alone pay for a flying lesson. I talk to my boss but he's not interested. I am frustrated as I am wasting my time and wasting my life. I go up to the chairman's office, walk in and sit down. He's a little taken aback and is visibly uncomfortable as he listens to my polite demands. "Ok Steve, I've got a job for you with a promotion and pay rise." I'm shocked that my plea has been agreed to so easily. Finally, selling high rate loans are behind me and I am now a vehicle repossession agent, a "repo man."

The pay increase is small but significant to me. I vow to save the extra money and spend it on finally getting my pilot's license. I am having coffee with my new supervisor, Carl, who is a retired policeman. He teaches me the art of legally breaking into cars. When our finance company determines that a debtor is unable to pay, we are sent to repossess the car to offset some of the debt. Unfortunately, we are a busy department. After we collect the car, I sell the car to one of several local dealers. For the carless debtor, a court summons demanding the balance will arrive within a couple of weeks. Of course, the company hopes to re-finance this debt at a high rate and start the cycle all over again. It's an unfriendly, cold and particularly unpleasant business. I am continually torn by the lack of ethics, especially as I see a lot of myself in many of the unfortunate borrowers' situations.

Most of the time, the debtor knows we are coming and they hand over the car keys without a fuss. Some have second thoughts when we arrive. One offered me a night with his wife in exchange for delaying the repossession by an extra two months! Sometimes, our credit collection department tells us to expect trouble based on their dealings with the debtor. That's the case today, which is why we are driving toward the customer's house before sunrise with large cups of coffee in our hands. The debtor has no idea we are coming. The only people we have informed are the local police. We are hoping that the car is parked in the street or in an unobstructed driveway. Carl has instructed me to wear dark clothes and not carry anything that "jangles." It is bitterly cold this morning and the roads are empty.

The car we are collecting is a gold BMW six-series. Car alarms are still relatively uncommon and Carl says that it will not be too tricky to unlock this car. I am thumbing through the documents as we arrive. The initial cost of the car was several thousand pounds. The amount owing is almost double the original cost once all the default fees are added. The debtor is thirty years old and has made sporadic payments since signing the loan. There have been no payments for the past two months and no responses to letters or phone calls. His occupation is listed as "crane operator" at the nearby shipyards. I wonder how this person is going to react when he finds his car missing. He will probably start with disbelief that somebody has "stolen" his car, turning to confusion when he realizes it was the finance company and then a great deal of anger. I hope that he is sleeping well as I don't want to see any of these emotions up close.

We pull into a dimly lit street and Carl spots the car. There are no obstructions around it. We park close to our target vehicle and I follow Carl. My cold breath is visible below an orange streetlight. He begins to pick the door lock. He signals me to watch. The door is open in a matter of seconds. The small vanity light illuminates inside. Carl works on the ignition next. In the quiet of the morning, my heart skips as the engine turns over and starts. Carl casually moves away without saying a word. I sit in the driver's seat. The debtor must be a big guy as the seat is very far back from the wheel. I fumble around to adjust it. My adrenaline is pumping, causing me to shake a little. Carl motions me to drive off and it's as simple as that. Only when I'm on a main road do I begin to breathe normally again. It is quite a rush.

During the past few months, I have become quite good at repossessing cars. I am also good at selling the recovered cars to local dealers. I learn their tricks and try to outwit them to get the maximum payout for the debtor. I have a good incentive too. My boss gives me 5% of any profit and that's extra money I am using to build my flying account. I volunteer to sell every car I can. I recently finished paying off my own car loan, which allows me to add a little more money to my flying account each month.

I am about to repossess my next car but this one is unusual. The car has been modified for a handicapped driver. I don't even think about the implications. I have been molded into the finance way of thinking, "the finance company was good enough to loan this person the money, an agreement was signed, and now they won't pay the money back." The fact that the vehicle is a lifeline for this person doesn't even cross my mind. The debtor has mailed the keys to us to prevent aggressive legal action and more fees. All I need to do is get in and drive off. It takes me a few minutes to work out how the various steering wheel levers control the car and I drive away. The route to the office takes me past my childhood home. My mother still lives there so I stop by but when she finds out what I am driving, she asks me to leave. Finally, the shame of what I am doing hits me as I drive off. My day gets worse when I arrive back at the finance company.

Unusually, the Chairman walks out to greet me. "Steve, we have a dealer on the way to look at that old Skoda," he says. "Sell it to him." I am slightly confused as the Skoda needs a new gearbox before we can sell it as it will not go in reverse. He sees my confusion. "We have pushed it back into the parking space, just don't let him put it in reverse and as soon as he signs for it, it'll be his problem." I'm not sure what to think and I don't have time as the friendly French dealer turns up within a few minutes. I'm still unsure about this but my mouth is on autopilot. I use the standard lines and play up the condition, the careful owner, and how clean the interior is. I avoid mentioning any mechanical issues. We go for a test drive. The little Skoda drives great forwards but I must stop him putting it in reverse. We get back to the finance company and he comes to a stop. "This is fine, you can leave it here," I say before he has any chance to back up. I can see the Chairman and another Director watching from their second story office window. I know what they are watching for, a handshake to seal the deal. I can almost hear the elation from the upstairs office when we finally shake. I feel sick. I like this dealer and I know I've sold him a piece of junk. I walk into the chairman's office and refuse any congratulations. I am just starting to find my feet and my flying account is beginning to build but I resign on the spot.

ISLAND FOG

Six months after resigning from the finance company I am finally back in the pilot's seat of a small aircraft. It still feels wonderful and I am itching to get airborne, but I will not fly today. I am being shown some small training aircraft at the flying school I have selected for my lessons. For almost an entire year, I have saved every spare penny I can. I work for a toy company as an Assistant Credit Manager, a recent promotion after initially beginning as a telephone debt collector. I wish that my flying career would move as quickly as my office career. I have enough money to buy ten hours of flight training and I want to start flying as soon as possible. As I sit in the comfortable cockpit of a small Grumman, the instructor talks about the aircraft, the rates and school rules. I hear none of it. Instead, I gaze out of the window and hold the controls, gently, just as I have been taught. I imagine myself soaring through the air with the aircraft and I begin to smile. "Smooth, smooth, smooth." We go back into the office and I book some lessons. I grab a coffee and chat to my new instructor, Mark.

He asks when I first became interested in flying. "It happened when I was eleven years old," I say as I recount the story. Thirty of my school friends and I are being told which lucky ten will go on a week-long trip to Guernsey, a small island near the coast of France. Our teacher has a box containing slips of paper with our names written on them. She has already pulled the first eight names and I have yet to hear my name. "Come on, come on," I keep repeating in my head. To be honest, any determination to go on the trip is simply fueled by wanting to get away from the monotony of this boring school. She pulls out the last two names and I'm not going. I sink into my chair, disappointed. Then, unexpected to all of us, she pulls out an eleventh name - my name! I am very confused. "You are the first reserve if somebody drops out." I look around at the ten selected pupils, wondering if any will pass up this chance to travel. I doubt that any of them will.

It is one week before my classmates leave for Guernsey and my teacher has given me a form for my parents to sign. It's an authorization form allowing me to travel on the trip; Kelvin has dropped out. I wait for the first strike of the school bell before running home quicker than I ever have before. I burst through the door at home and hand the form over to my parents with no breath left to explain. I can't believe it when they hand it back to me. The cost of the trip is £120, money my parents simply do not have. I feel deflated and take the news quite badly. I go to bed, grumpy. I can hear my parents talking downstairs but I can't make out what they are saying. It is late but I hear my dad leave. The next morning, they hand me the signed note and enough money to cover the trip. I am so thankful but I don't hang around long enough to ask questions. I suspect a last-minute loan has just added to our family debt but I am thrilled.

This is the first time that I have traveled away from home. The luxury bus has velvet curtains in the windows and a polished wooden table in front of my seat. I feel like a rock star! We arrive at Eastleigh Airport for the one-hour flight to Guernsey. I climb the small metal steps protruding from the cabin door and board a dark blue Handley Page Herald airliner. It has forty seats, a high wing and two large propellers. I sit next to an oval window on the left side and put on my seatbelt. I can clearly see the engine and wheel strut underneath the long wing. The left engine begins to start. I see a flash of fire come from the exhaust pipe and then the propeller spins up. The pilots start the other engine and we taxi out towards the runway. I am quite fascinated by the moving parts outside of my window during the takeoff The propellers have condensation coming from the tips as they speed up and there are large flaps moving around the back of the wing before the wheels retract into the bottom of the engines. It's all so captivating that I don't really appreciate that we are airborne until I gaze down at the world moving below us. Soon, we are above a layer of clouds and there is nothing more for me to see. The high pitch drone of the engines are ever present and every now and then we are bumped around. I do not pay too much attention to the flight. My thoughts are focused on our destination and thinking about what the hotel might look like.

A voice comes over the loudspeaker, it's the captain. He says that there is bad weather in Guernsey, so we are going to land at a neighboring island and wait for the fog to clear. I am a little disappointed as this delay will eat into our trip. The stewardess comes through to check our seat belts are tight. As soon as she passes me, I unbuckle again so that I can look down through my window. We are in the clouds. Raindrops are beading back across the window. I am keen to see the ground and the new world I suspect will be different to my home, but all I can see is cloud. I hear the engine note change several times and large flaps extend at the back of the wing. Still, I see nothing but cloud. Next, a loud "clunk" and the wheels come down from their pods under the engine. I still cannot see a thing, just a lot of rain and dark clouds. I stare harder.

I start to wonder if the pilot's will ever be able to find the runway but we continue down. The whole experience is beginning to intrigue me. We continue down and down with no sight of any land. Where is the runway? And then, I witness the most incredible sight. No more than a few seconds before we touch down, the cloud disappears and the runway pops into view for our landing. "Welcome to Jersey." I barely hear the arrival announcements over the noise in my brain. I didn't even realize that we had parked and the propellers had stopped turning. I didn't know that I was the last person on the plane. I am still quite baffled. I can't stop thinking about how the pilots found the runway and landed safely with the thick cloud all around us. How on earth did they know where the runway was?

One of the teachers grabs me and ushers me towards the open door at the back of the cabin but I want to go forward. I want to get to the pilots and ask my million questions. As I walk across the foggy apron, I catch a glimpse of the captain. He sees me looking and waves. This is the moment that it happened. The sights, sounds, mystery and magic of flying have entered my bloodstream for good. Aviation begins to take over my every thought. We eventually make it to Guernsey and we spend several days exploring the sights but I really don't remember too much of these days. However, I remember the short flight from Jersey to Guernsey in detail. I ensure I get a window seat for our flight home to Southampton too, so that I can absorb every movement and every sound. I crave technical knowledge of these amazing flying machines. I am hooked for life.

SOLO SMIFFY

I left the toy company just over one year ago after I was offered a promotion as Credit Manager for a national convenience store chain. I have just turned twenty-three years old. I have a good salary and a new credit card in my wallet. The high credit limit surprises me but it tells me I am beginning to turn a corner with my finances. My bank account balance is still pitiful but I can afford to eat now. At the flying school, the person behind the desk swipes my card and I buy five more flying lessons. I am overjoyed that I will get to fly every weekend for the next few weeks. I can afford to meet the minimum credit card payments each month and I really don't care how long it takes to pay back the balance. My airline career is waiting for me and I am conscious that time is continuing to tick by. After I finish my flying lesson today, I will have logged ten hours. That will leave just thirty hours remaining before I can take my flight test and receive my pilot's license. Then I'll apply to the airlines and pay off my debt. I head out into the cold English winter for another lesson.

Martin has been my instructor for the last few flying hours. He goes by his nickname of "Smiffy." We are getting on well and I really like the small 4-seat Grumman Cheetah I'm flying. We have spent the last two lessons flying round and round the airport, repeatedly taking-off and landing. At first, Smiffy gave a running commentary, telling me everything I needed to do, but during the last lesson he was very quiet. He didn't say too much at all and so I just got on with flying round and round the airport. Perhaps he is getting bored? My landings are quite good now. Initially, I had trouble with landing as they were always a little firm or on one wheel first. Smiffy always had something to say about my early attempts; "blimey, were we shot down!" or "that's right, get two landings for the price of one!" But there was one landing last week that really worked out well, something "clicked", and it's been so much easier ever since. I now feel totally in control, as if the wheels are attached to me, and I know exactly where they are going to touch the runway. I am expecting some more good landings today.

It is 16th December 1994 and it is bitterly cold outside. Smiffy has stayed in the warm clubhouse while I scrape a little frost from the top of the Grumman wing. I can see him watching me as I complete my pre-flight checks. He is drinking coffee. I check the oil, fuel, control surfaces and then get into the cockpit to begin the pre-start procedures. I'm especially glad we are in this Cheetah today, registration **G-OMOG**. The heater works well in "Oscar Golf." Smiffy gets into the seat next to me. "I'm not feeling great," he says. I'm concerned as he really doesn't seem right. "We don't have to fly," I say but he motions me to continue. We are about to take off for some more circuits around the airport. Before I apply the power, I glance across at Smiffy. He is staring out of the window and doesn't seem to be interested in what I am doing. I go through my normal routine around the pattern, trying to keep my movements extra smooth for the sake of Smiffy. As I make the second approach to landing, he groans. "Get on the ground, just taxi straight to the tower." This is really concerning to me. I concentrate to make a smooth landing without screwing up. For his sake, I can't afford to go-around and do it again. I go through my same procedure: speed is 75 knots, power is set, flaps are down, and my descent rate is stable. The landing is nice, but it doesn't really matter to me this time. I taxi to the tower as quickly as I can and stop. I reach for the mixture control to stop the engine but Smiffy stops me from pulling it. I am confused. He turns, smiles and giggles. "I'm fine, but I'm getting out! I wanted to make sure you could fly without really thinking about it." It was a devious ploy. Smiffy has distracted me to see if I could keep flying my procedures while he diverted my attention. My reward is an authorization to fly my first solo flight. Smiffy jumps out of the Grumman as if miraculously healed. "Do three around the pattern and come back, I'll be watching."

This is it. I have a total of ten hours of training, five in the Chipmunk and five in the Cheetah. I really feel at home in G-OMOG. I close the canopy knowing that I can do this. Smiffy has confidence in me and I don't want to let him down. I am taxiing out to runway 02 at Eastleigh Airport in the south of England. It is a familiar route but it feels very different doing it by myself. It is much roomier in the small cabin without Smiffy next to me. I spread out my elbows and enjoy the extra space. I stop just before the runway to do my engine checks, the same way I have for the last few flights. I am ready. I take a breath; I want to take this all in. I look around the airport.

The first Supermarine Spitfire flew from this exact location 58 years ago. The Spitfire I was admiring when I first discovered the *Air Training Corps* flew from this very runway. The Handley Page Herald airliner I first flew in, on our school trip many years ago, flew from this runway. I have spent many skipped school days and workdays watching aircraft fly from this runway during the past decade and now here I am, me, about to fly my first solo flight from this same historic runway. I am conscious that I am taking too long but I'm lost in the moment. I don't want Smiffy to think that I'm having second thoughts and so I taxi onto the runway.

It is 11:35am. I push the throttle forward and the little Grumman starts moving down the runway. I keep it nailed to the centerline with smooth rudder movements. Without Smiffy on board, the Grumman is lighter and things happen much quicker than I'm used to. There's 60 knots, ease back on the wheel and I am airborne! I cannot stop my grin but I try to concentrate. My heart io racing. "Attitude correct, speed is 79 knots, smooth, smooth, smooth." I watch the red radar antenna pass by my right wing in my peripheral. I see the green grass surrounding the far end of the runway and the railway tracks beyond. I want to remember this flight forever. "How high am I? How are the engine temperatures and pressures?" All is good. I go through my standard routine, just as I have been doing for the past few lessons. I talk through each step out loud to myself. I absolutely love this. Soon enough, I am lined up with the runway for my first solo landing. I am determined to make this a good one. "Looking nice, checks are done, speed is good, flaps coming down, and I'm ready." I find myself with slightly white knuckles as I near the runway. "Relax," I tell myself. I reduce the power and start to feel for the touchdown. I sense that I am a part of the little Cheetah and every control input I make gets the exact response I expect. The wheels gently touch down, it's by far the best landing I have ever made! I have done it. It is the most significant day of my life so far. "Oh, my God, I am a pilot!" The far end of the runway is getting closer. "Oh shit," I remember that I'm still moving. I raise the flaps, put on full power and I'm off again for my second flight around the pattern. There is no looking back now.

STEALING TIME

It is dark, cold and raining hard. I am hiding in some damp bushes with my new boss Rob. After spending six months as Credit Manager, I was offered a job as a Loss Prevention Manager for our company. It came with a pay-rise, which I intend to spend on flying. I am part of a small team charged with investigating theft for about 1,000 convenience stores throughout the United Kingdom. Our focus is theft by store staff, which can be far costlier to the company than general shoplifting. Tonight, we are trying to catch a thief in the act. It started raining a few minutes ago but these bushes give us the best view of the convenience store back door. After analyzing stock paperwork, our team spotted an ever-increasing discrepancy in the number of cigarettes being ordered against those being sold. I visited the store a few days ago and managed to get a tip-off from another staff member. Now, we need to see it for ourselves. I hope we are not going to be disappointed as Rob and I are already soaked from the rain.

"This is so glamorous," Rob chuckles. Then, across the parking lot, the back door of the store opens. From the shadows, several people move towards the light and we can see somebody handing out stacks of boxes. "Are they cigarettes?" Rob asks. I move over to get a better look. "Yep, that's it." We move in, dripping wet. The people quickly scatter back into the shadows as we approach. We catch the evening supervisor red-handed. After a short interview, she is arrested and walked through the store to the waiting police car. We make sure that the store staff clearly sees this and we know that the news will spread quickly. We won't have to visit this store again for quite a while. Sadly, there are plenty more stores with theft problems waiting for our visit.

There are two main ways we discover theft in our stores: paperwork discrepancies or a tip-off from a store employee. I spend many long evenings studying stock numbers, bank statements and sales receipts to find patterns of possible theft. If I find anything suspicious, I visit the store and pretend to be a customer, slowly filling a basket for twenty minutes while I try to get a feel for what might be going on. I take note of everything I see and I try to identify any honest looking employees to discuss my concerns. I often follow my "gut feel" when selecting a staff member to confide in and it is rarely wrong.

Most of the honest staff know who the likely thief in their store is, but they are usually reluctant to talk for fear of losing their own job or suffering retaliation. I feel for them and understand. Most of our stores are in poorer neighborhoods, similar to where I grew up. Everyone knows everyone else and everyone knows everyone else's business. A "snitch" is the worst label to have in such a small community. My toughest job is to win the confidence of the staff member and convince them that their identity will never be revealed. It is usually a very hard sell. Sometimes, I suspect the store Manager, especially in cases where cash is missing. In those cases, I'll often try to find somebody in the store whom I suspect to be a petty thief: the odd packet of cigarettes, the odd bottle of vodka, the odd twenty-pound note. I interview this person while the Manager is out of the store and encourage a shift of our focus away from the petty thieving and towards the main thief. These tactics usually reveal enough details to build a quick case and catch the Manager in the act.

Rob and I are at another store in the south of England. It's 3am, before anyone has turned up for work, and none of the staff know that we are here. We have been reliably informed that the Manager is stealing large amounts of cash and "cooking" the books to cover his tracks. Apparently, the Manager goes to a locked stock room to hide his stolen cash in trash bags. He then "takes out the trash" all the way to his car. We need to stop this quickly and our chosen tool is a tiny hidden video camera. Rob makes a little hole in the ceiling tile and mounts the camera above it. I find a suitable place above the ceiling struts for the video recording equipment and run the cables. Installing this equipment is something we have done many times before and we are finished within an hour.

We go back to the store during normal hours the following week. Some members of staff immediately recognize us; there have been theft issues at this store before. We begin by interviewing the Manager. He is uncomfortable but pronounces his innocence. My gut tells me that he is lying and Rob knows it too. The Manager is sweating, fidgeting and nervous. Near the end of the interview, we tell him about the hidden camera. He still refuses to confess and I wonder if he thinks we are bluffing. There's only one thing left to do. I get a small stepladder, push up the ceiling tile in the stock room and retrieve the videotape.

I sit with Rob and the Manager in a back office, ready to play the videotape on a small black and white monitor. Rob gives the Manager one last chance to confess but he doesn't. I push play and begin looking for movement. On the small screen, we see the

Manager walk into the stock room. I am hoping we will see the stolen cash go into the trash bag as it's the only way we will be able to prove the case without a confession. But, we are surprised at what we see next. Following the Manager into the stock room is a young lady, the night supervisor. We never suspected two people might be involved. We watch closely, waiting for any sign of the stolen cash. Then, the female begins to undress! I look up at the Manager. He has his head fully buried in his hands. I look back at the screen in time to see them begin to kiss and we stop the tape. I am lost for words. "Just don't tell my wife," the Manager pleads. Knowing that we still don't have evidence of the cash theft, Rob asks for his resignation. He leaves the store and promises never to return in exchange for the tape being deleted. A new Manager is soon put in charge and I know that not a penny will ever go missing from this store again.

Despite my unusual profession, the freedom of travel that my job gives me is wonderful. I enjoy being out of the office and driving around England, Scotland and Wales. I always make time to find a new airfield and always like to stop for lunch. It is great to sit and chat to other people who have the "flying bug." Today, I stop off at a little grass airfield in the medieval town of Salisbury in the south of England. As I sip my coffee, a bubbly man sits down next to me and asks if I want to fly! Within ten minutes I am airborne with Larry in his pretty little two seat Bulldog. What a wonderful machine. This is the aircraft that replaced the Chipmunk as the RAF basic trainer, and I can see why. It is much more powerful than the Chipmunk or Cheetah. "Do you like aerobatics?" Larry asks. I don't have time to answer as we are already upside down and Larry is grinning from ear to ear. When we land, Larry tells me that he expects nothing in return, except an acknowledgment that I have enjoyed the experience. I really have!

There are more cheerful people like Larry and Old Sarum Airfield seems much friendlier than some I have visited before. The airfield is also quite close to my home. I am told that it is the oldest continuoucly operating airfield in the world, having been constructed in 1917. The huge wartime hangars are historically preserved buildings and are magnificent. There are several monuments to past significant aviation events dotted around the airfield. Old Sarum played a part in both World Wars and was designated as the first training base for the newly founded Royal Air Force on its inception day in April 1918. At the end of the grass runway are the ruins of a medieval castle dating from the 11th Century, built on a hilltop constructed around 600BC. I really get a sense of the incredible history as I walk around. I like this place a lot; it just feels right. I check the flying rates and find that they are cheaper than at Eastleigh. My logbook has fifteen hours in it and I have flown solo for two hours. I am desperate to fly again. I decide to come back and finish up my pilot's license here.

I decide to work hard and pay down some of my credit card debt. The interest has been soaring more than I have. A few months of determined extra payments should help to bring the balance down and then I'll start flying again at Old Sarum. I drive away from the airfield in a determined mood, heading towards my next store thief.

LOW FLYING

It is one month later and I am following my plan of slowly paying down the interest on my debts. My aunt has asked me to stop by and see her, so I am sitting in her dimly lit room in a chair opposite her. I have always been close to my aunt but something is weird this time. She has never asked me to stop by like this before. I tell her about my solo flying and my airline ambitions. She loves the idea of traveling and has been planning her retirement trip for as many years as I can remember. She is due to retire next month and has almost finalized the plans for her trip around the world. She will travel alone as she never married and often prefers her own company; we have that in common. She's the most frugal person I know and has saved just about every penny she has ever earned. I start asking about her trip but something is wrong. The conversation stops.

She takes a breath. "There won't be a trip, I have cancer." I can't believe what I am hearing and I have no idea what to say or how to react. She doesn't look sick. She leans toward me and grabs my arm firmly. "Don't you ever do what I did," she says. "I wasted my whole life saving for this stupid trip, and I'm not going to be able to take it. Please, promise me that you will live your life now, and enjoy it before it's too late." A few weeks later, she is dead. I do not go to her funeral as I prefer to remember her alive, but my outlook on life and my attitude towards money has changed forever. My new plan is to enjoy my life to the fullest and stop worrying about money or material things. If I am gifted a normal lifetime, I will judge the success of my life by my experiences and achievements, not by the size of my bank account when I die.

I am not waiting around anymore. Screw the debt, life is passing me by and saving a bunch of money will be useless to me if I pass away before I can achieve my dream. I take out a bank loan and apply for another credit card. I enroll at a professional pilot college and I am thrilled when ten large aviation technical books turn up on my doorstep. I quickly settle into my new routine. When I am not investigating theft, I am flying at Old Sarum. In the evenings, I study my aviation books until I fall asleep. I love Old Sarum and I still see Larry often, always with a smile on his face. We usually end up flying around in his Bulldog for a few minutes. Larry is very encouraging about my career ambitions and he loves my new attitude. He reminds me of that first impromptu flight we took and tells me I must take people flying when I own my own aircraft. I agree, but I remind him that it's incredibly unlikely I will ever be able to own a plane as I can barely afford to own a skateboard!

My instructor at Old Sarum is Kim, a funny and attractive lady who is building hours to become an airline pilot. She is an excellent instructor who allows me just enough room to screw something up and just enough time to fix it before she intervenes. The aircraft I am flying is unusual. It's a Slingsby T67, used by several overseas military organizations as a training aircraft, but it is quite rare in England. It has two side-by-side seats, a low wing and it's aerobatic. It has a stick to fly, just like the Chipmunk and the Bulldog. The Slingsby is very responsive and has great visibility through a large bulbous canopy. I "click" with the little Slingsby very quickly and some consistent good landings follow, which means it isn't too long before I am back to flying around the pattern on my own. I savor every minute I can spend in the air. I am having a blast, despite my mounting debt and depleting bank account balance.

A few months later, I am sitting alone in the Slingsby having just completed a navigation exercise that involved planning and flying to two other airfields in the south of England. This is what flying small planes is all about to me: the freedom of flight and discovering new places. It is so much fun and particularly satisfying when an airfield comes into view exactly where I plan it to be. My aunt left me a small amount of money after she died, which went straight into my flying account to pay for the last twenty flying hours I have flown. Things are starting to happen quickly. Before I know it, I am ready to take my flight test and I feel confident. Kim has prepared me very well and I can still hear her voice in my head as I begin to taxi out with the examiner sitting next to me.

It is 28th August 1996 at 7:35pm, a sunny English day. I have just landed Slingsby **G-BJNG** and taxied to the parking area at Old Sarum. I pull the mixture control to cut the fuel supply and the engine goes quiet. Simon, the examiner sitting next to me, is quiet too. I look at him for any sign of news, good or bad. He is completely deadpan. What is going on? He can't hold it anymore and finally smiles. Ten years and two months after I first sat in that RAF Chipmunk, I am a fully qualified pilot.

Aviation has taken over my whole life. I am doing well with my professional pilot studies and I am thoroughly enjoying the learning experience. I continue to work to meet my loan payments each month but any spare money is quickly spent on flying an hour here and an hour there. I am slowly gaining experience, flying different types of aircraft all over England. To keep challenging myself, I have flown complex, tail wheel, aerobatic and high performance aircraft with some wonderful pilot friends. Many aircraft owners see a little of my enthusiasm and offer to take me flying. For me, every hour in my logbook is precious.

One pilot friend teaches me a great deal. Peter is a former air-race pilot and owns a beautiful red Italian Falco. It looks every bit the sports car of the sky with gorgeous flowing lines, just like the Spitfire. Peter and I fly together often and I love it when he shares some of his air-racing experience with me. Today, we are heading out away from houses to find some trees in an empty field we will use as pretend race pylons. We are flying low and fast, it is very exciting and I can see the concentration in his face. Peter shows me how to manage the energy of the Falco during the turn, taking the straightest line to avoid losing too much speed within our imaginary course. It takes a great deal of focus to fly this accurately but Peter is a master and tells me the key is to fly as smoothly as possible. It seems to be a common theme in all the flying I do. With some practice, I can soon replicate his tight lines around the trees and he is happy with my progress. I am thrilled when we land and the "buzz" takes many hours to wear off.

I look forward to my weekends when I can fly family and friends around the south of England. I split the costs equally between me and my passengers, which helps to keep the flying bills lower. My logbook is slowly filling up and my experience level is growing. I am determined to keep building my hours and be competitive for an airline position once the industry starts hiring again. I have 130 hours of flying time in my logbook. I've had my share of good and bad landings, but I am never embarrassed to go-around and try again if an approach looks bad. My confidence and comfort level are both extremely high. I feel completely in control of every different type of aircraft I fly. One short flight is about to change all of that.

I am finishing lunch with friends I have flown to the Isle of Wight, a small island twenty miles south of the English coast. I love to bring people here as it feels like we have really traveled somewhere. The only other way to reach the island is by a forty-minute ferry ride. It's not a perfect day to fly, but it's nice enough. There are spots of sunshine around a few low clouds. I must avoid the clouds on our flight back to Old Sarum as I am not yet qualified to fly in them. One of my passengers is Keith, who owns the company that supplies some of the security cameras we use for theft prevention. He is in good spirits, as is his wife Gill and their daughter Mandy. The lunch is tasty, a proper English "Sunday roast" of beef, roasted potatoes and gravy. As we walk out to the little four-seat Robin aircraft, I gaze up at the cloudy sky. It is hard to judge just how low the clouds are and so I suggest that we go up and take a quick look. If the clouds are too low, we will come back and wait for them to dissipate. The little four-seat Robin is reasonably roomy but we are still quite cozy sitting together in the cabin. Before we reach 600 feet, the clouds touch the canopy and so I descend to stay below the layer, turn back towards the airfield and land. I am happy with my decision, although a little embarrassed that I'm not able to fly into the clouds to get us home.

As the day progresses, the clouds seem to get lower and lower. This is not what I saw when I checked the weather this morning. The only guarantee that an English weather forecast seems to offer is no guarantees! The final decision is easy for me to make; we will go to a hotel for the night and fly back home tomorrow. Our quick lunch flight is becoming quite the adventure, especially as none of us have brought a change of clothes. Much laughter is generated because of our unusual predicament. Luckily, the hotel has enough "emergency" toothpaste and deodorant for all of us.

I sleep well and a sausage, bacon and egg breakfast in the small hotel restaurant starts the day well. We head out to the airfield and I begin to do my pre-flight checks on the Robin. I check the fuel quantity, oil quantity, control surfaces and tires. The weather is like it was yesterday but the clouds look a little bit higher. I check with the weather people again. The outlook is better and the staff back at Old Sarum say they are already in clear skies. I only need the cloud base to be above 1,000 feet so that I can safely navigate across the water and back to the mainland. Another small plane lands and parks close by. Keith and I walk over and chat to the pilot. "Oh, it's not too bad, just a bit "scuddy" in places." Based on this news, we board up; Keith sits up front and Gill and Mandy are in the back. Soon enough, the engine is warm and I open the throttle to start my takeoff run. We lift off easily in the cool morning air. I look around for the first signs of a cloud base. It is a little more turbulent today. We are at 800 feet before the base of the clouds touch the canopy. It's slightly lower than I'd like but I decide to continue, expecting the conditions to improve as we fly.

There are only 20 miles of water between us and the coast of England and it will only take 15 minutes to cross. At least I know the height of the English Channel; there are no mountains to hit across the channel. I am concentrating hard on the murky horizon in front of me. Unexpectedly, the visibility is deteriorating as I fly north. The horizon is blending into a fuzzy border between the mist below and the cloud above. Some more clouds envelop the canopy again and I head down a little more to stay clear. I'm at 600ft now, which makes me a little uncomfortable. I wonder when the good weather will appear; it should be clear at any moment. I estimate that we are half way across the Channel but the clouds are still forcing me lower and I can feel my heart rate increase as I try to think. How low can I go? Where is this good weather? Just at the worst possible time, the turbulence increases significantly and violently bounces our little Robin up and down. My concentration is now split between trying to stay below the clouds and staying as level as I can without a good horizon to reference.

I can hear the two girls shriek in the back with every bump. They know we are in trouble but they are trying to keep as quiet as they can to allow me to concentrate. I look back briefly and see the look of terror in their faces. They are holding each other's hands as tightly as they can. Keith points to our altitude. I'm already aware that we are now only 200ft above the water. This is crazy; I can't believe that I am doing this. The visibility drops even more and the rain starts hitting the canopy. I can barely see ahead. My mind is racing and I'm trying to focus. I don't think I can safely turn around without losing control and I believe we must be so close to the coast. I am stuck in the worst position I can imagine. Where is this better weather? Where is the coastline? I physically jump when I see a large red channel buoy pass just below my left wing. I'm down at the level of the ships. "Shit, I am way too low."

The girls begin to panic now, screaming with every bump. Keith has a look of horror on his face. I begin to think that we might not have much time left. This was supposed to be a pleasure flight and instead I am putting these people through hell. I must clear my head and think. "Fly the plane," I tell myself. "Aviate, navigate, communicate," I keep repeating to myself in a calm voice. Of course, communicate! I remember the frequency for Eastleigh Airport from my solo flying days. I call them up and tell the controller I am in trouble. I am trying to sound calm but I know my voice is trembling with fear. I stop short of using the word "emergency," simply to prevent more panic from my unfortunate passengers. "We have you in radar contact. Turn right, heading 010." It is a lifeline. I ignore everything else and concentrate on accurately flying the heading. At last, the cloud begins to slowly lift and I follow the base up. Soon, the horizon returns and we start to see spots of land ahead. Keith points it out, overjoyed. Gill begins to cry, letting out the emotion of her ordeal.

We land on runway 02 at Eastleigh. I feel completely drained, embarrassed and a complete failure. I can't believe that I have put these good people though such a terrifying experience. I am confused by their praise. "You were great, we are safe," Keith says. He shakes my hand. Gill and Mandy hug me. They are both wiping tears but smiling. I am baffled. I was the one that caused all of this with my poor decision-making. I feel like a total imposter. As they leave, I go to the café, order a coffee and find a seat away from everyone else. I talk to myself, wrestling with the question of whether I should ever fly again. It takes me almost an hour to decide on a plan. I write an entry into my logbook, the words are shaky from the adrenaline. "Low clouds, scared, diverted, need instrument rating." I draw a line under the entry. Before I ever take passengers again, I will learn to fly in the clouds.

GO WEST

For the past few years, I have been wearing "disposable" contact lenses to sharpen up my vision. I am having a check-up with my optician today. He has some bad news for me. My eyesight is getting worse and my eye health is deteriorating. He and I both know why. To save a little money, I have a terrible habit of leaving the same contact lenses in for several days at a time instead of replacing the costly lenses with new ones. I rarely remove them to sleep too. It's an unhealthy practice he has heard from his patients before and he explains that cutting off oxygen to my eyes will eventually damage them permanently. "Why don't you fix this for good," he says. Laser correction is relatively new but he believes it is safe and I am a good candidate. He believes that the improvement to my eye health will outweigh the risks and so I call my good friend Andy, who is a respected eye surgeon. We talk for hours about the risks and benefits and I ultimately make the decision to fix my eyes. I'm sad that this corrective surgery wasn't available when I applied to fly with the Royal Air Force, but at least I'll have the chance to join the airlines with perfect eyesight.

I am waiting in a small medical office in the north of England opposite a girl who is about the same age as me. We are both here to have the LASIK eye correction procedure. I chose this place because of their "buy one eye, get one free" offer! I am terrified but she seems quite calm as she reads a magazine. I introduce myself and we begin to chat. I don't want to let her know that I am seriously considering changing my mind. After a few minutes, the nurse comes into the room and calls her name. Suddenly, the girl starts to panic. I try my best to calm her. "There is nothing to worry about, this is a quick and safe procedure," I say. "Go on, you won't regret it, it's such an easy procedure, you'll be done before you know it." She listens, nods, and goes into the surgery room with the nurse. After convincing her to go through with the procedure, I know that I can't back out now. The nurse comes back into the room and asks me to put my head back, which enables her to put some anesthetic drops into my eye. It's too late to stop her and before I know it I am lying on a surgical table with the laser machine above my right eye. I should be shaking but I am literally frozen with fear. The machine moves around above my eye and I brace myself for the pain. "Ok, now for the next eye," the surgeon says. I'm stunned, I didn't feel anything, there was no pain. Within five minutes, the procedure is complete and I am given dark glasses to wear, as the nurse helps me into a dimly lit recovery room to join the girl.

I am too scared to blink or move my eyes around. My eyeballs feel a little strange, like having a small piece of grit in them. I slowly look around the sparse room. There is a picture of some red flowers on the wall and dark green curtains keep the sunlight out. In the corner of the room is an electric fan with a black wire grill cover. The fan is not plugged in. What happens next stuns me. As I stare at the fan, the individual strands of wire on the grill begin to come into focus. At first, I don't believe what I am seeing and I gently close my eyes. When I look again, I watch the grill come into sharp focus over a two-minute period. It is the most incredible thing I have ever seen. Thirty minutes later, I go up some stairs and into a small room for an eye test. Both the girl and I have perfect vision as we leave.

Six months later, my eyes are healed and things are back to normal at home. My girlfriend is giving me a hard time about the amount of money I am spending on flying. Truthfully, she is more concerned about the debt I am accumulating, which is understandable. Because of this, and the fact that I spend every evening studying for my airline exams, we are not getting along very well. I don't blame her for being pissed off, but I really need to keep studying. I am due to sit twelve different technical aviation exams in a few months and I'm determined to pass.

My good friend is a captain at Virgin Atlantic Airlines. Dave flies the magnificent Boeing 747. He suggests I join him and go to America to build some more flying time and experience. The current exchange rate makes flying in the USA almost half price for me. He offers a discount "staff travel" flight with him to Los Angeles. I have plenty of vacation time owed to me and so it's a very easy decision to make. I do some research and find a good flight school in San Diego. The Federal Aviation Administration (FAA) regulates all flying in America and so I decide to challenge myself a little instead of just building hours flying around in circles. "Is it possible to convert to an FAA multi-engine, commercial and instrument rating in 3 weeks?" There is a long pause and it's not from the regular telephone satellite delay between the UK and America. "Man, that's quite a tall order, you'd kinda have to fly a whole bunch of hours every day and night."

The flight with Dave to Los Angeles is incredible. I am sitting in the cockpit of the 747, soaking up the entire experience; every noise, light, bump and piece of paper intrigues me. Seeing the iceberg flows from Greenland and the sun set over the Atlantic Ocean for the first time is mesmerizing. I follow the busy arrival into

Los Angeles using a chart and soon after we head out with the crew for a party. It is such good fun and I feel that I am glimpsing a little bit of my future life. I'm keen to drive the two hours to San Diego in the morning and get airborne. The next day, I arrive into the beautiful southern California city of San Diego. It is sunny and warm; very different to England. My first stop is the FAA medical examiner's office. My English medical and flying license are not valid for flying aircraft registered with the FAA. The examiner asks about my laser correction as he is thinking about having the procedure done too. He tests my eyesight and finds that my vision is still better than 20/20. More importantly, I can tell that my eyes are healthier and less irritated. He issues an unrestricted first class medical, the highest level the FAA can issue and one that is required for all airline pilots in the United States. I stop at a flying supplies store nearby, buy a bunch of books and some new maps. I am ready to start flying tomorrow and go to bed with excited anticipation.

A few days later, I am completing the pre-flight checks on the small two-engine Beech Duchess at Montgomery Field in San Diego. I flew the Duchess in England and I enjoy its harmonized controls and solid feel. My instructor, Mike, has just finished giving me another thorough ground briefing. He is a good instructor and my flying training has been going well. The most challenging part for me has been learning the different radio procedures, using unfamiliar maps and understanding the regulations used in America. Despite these differences the Duchess flies the same way in both English and American air. One new skill I must learn is how to fly in mountainous areas. The highest mountain in the whole of the United Kingdom rises around 4,000ft. To the east of San Diego are peaks rising to 7,000ft. Luckily for me, Mike is an expert and I soak up his knowledge like a sponge. His lessons are fascinating, fun and challenging. Mike has a plan to get me through my multi-engine test, instrument test and commercial pilot test within my 3-week stay. We will dedicate one-week of solid training to each element, with a flight test coming at the end of each week. We fly from morning until late into each evening and I am having a blast. I am so glad that I decided to empty my bank account and come here and I'm sure my late aunt would approve.

My three weeks are almost done and I have successfully completed both my FAA multi-engine test and instrument test. Tomorrow is my commercial flight test but today I am seated in the back of the Duchess. Joe, the FAA examiner who administered my other tests, is in the front with another student. He has invited me to watch a test like the one I will take tomorrow. The engines are already running and I am getting comfortable in the back seat. His candidate student has missed a couple of minor items on the checklist but Joe doesn't seem too worried. I pay close attention to every radio call, responding in my head for practice. We takeoff and all is going well. The student makes a right turn and we head north, as planned. We will make another right turn towards the practice area next. A few minutes go by but the student hasn't turned. I glance at my map to check our position. Joe fidgets in his seat and I look at my map again. "Oh no," I realize why Joe is so uncomfortable with this error. The restricted airspace of Naval Air Station Miramar is a few miles ahead of us. This is a big mistake and I hope the student will turn soon. We do not have a clearance to enter Miramar and I wonder how far Joe will let this go. "Are you happy with your current position?" he says to the student. There is a pause. "Yes," he says. "NO," I say in my head! Another pause. We are getting very close to Miramar now. "So, you are definitely happy with your position?" Joe is really trying to help him out but I suspect that this will be his last chance. The student pauses and looks at the map again. "Yes," he says. "I have control," Joe says as he turns the Duchess sharply to the right. The test is over in a matter of minutes. It is a sobering experience and I hardly sleep, wondering if I could make a similar blunder when I am in the pilot's seat tomorrow morning.

Two days later, I am back in the cockpit jump-seat of the Boeing 747 with Dave in the captain's seat flying me back to England. My freshly signed FAA commercial, multi, instrument pilot's license is in my back pocket. I am ecstatic that I could achieve my goal with a lot of hard work and with help from the instructors in San Diego. My trip to America has been a thoroughly enjoyable and a valuable experience, but as we fly through the darkness towards home, my thoughts turn to studying for my English commercial pilot's license, the one I will need to fly for an airline in England. I am extremely proud of my FAA pilot's license but it will not get me a job in Europe. When I get home, I put my American license into a drawer believing I will never use it again.

IRISH LUCK

A letter has just arrived at home. I take it upstairs as I want to be alone when I open it. These are my exam results from the UK Civil Aviation Authority (CAA) airline pilot tests. It has been two weeks since I spent two grueling days at Gatwick Airport taking the twelve technical exams. It will take me months to save enough money to re-sit any failed tests but I know that it is unusual to pass all the exams on the first attempt. I take a deep breath and slowly open the letter:

Navigation PASS, Flight Planning, PASS,
Instruments PASS, Meteorology PASS,
Aviation Law PASS, Human Performance PASS,
Principles of Flight PASS, Morse Code PASS,
Airframe/Systems/Powerplant PASS, Mass & Balance PASS,
Aircraft Performance PASS, Operations Procedures PASS

I am absolutely elated. I have passed all twelve on the first attempt! It is a milestone and there is simply no stopping me now. I call my friend Les to share the great news. Les is a captain at a new Irish airline and he has been monitoring my career progress. I know he wants me to attend an interview after I pass my tests. Les was my age when he decided to change career and follow his passion into commercial airline flying. It took him several years of hard work but he is now a senior captain and has a very good life. He is a great inspiration for me to continue. In fact, I remember talking to him in his kitchen several months ago, at a time when I was losing faith in ever being able to start my airline career. It was a real low point for me and my debt was spiraling out of control despite the great flying experience I was gaining. Everything seemed to be taking far too long and I was pouring so much money into my flying that I knew I would soon have to stop and do something else. I also watched several friends start their airline and military flying jobs. I was happy for each of them but it also tugged at a nerve and made me realize just how far behind I was. "Perhaps it would be easier to do something else, something more normal," I said to Les. In response, he made me a cup of coffee and proceeded to give me a verbal kick in the ass. "Don't you waste what you've already achieved, you are on the right track and you'll regret it forever if you quit now," he said. Les told me of his financial struggles when he was in my position. "I used to hide when the rent collector came to the door," he said with his wry smile. "I made it work, why not you too?" In true airline pilot fashion, he came up with a plan and we sat for almost an hour as he mapped out a realistic path to the co-pilot seat of the Boeing 737 at his airline. Passing the written exams was the first major task he gave me to complete.

I call him up and he offers his congratulations. Les explains that flying for an Irish carrier will include some additional steps. Like the exclusivity of the CAA and FAA licenses, I will need to convert my flying license to an Irish Aviation Authority (IAA) version before I can officially start a job with his airline. The expense of adding an IAA license to my American and English licenses is frustrating, especially as I will be flying an American built aircraft and be based in England! I hate the bureaucracy but I have little choice except jump through the hoops as things finally seem to be moving with my career. I enroll at an Irish flying school just outside of Dublin and quickly begin my conversion course. I will be spending much of my time in Ireland and so I quit my job at the convenience store so that I can concentrate on flying. Things move very quickly after this and soon my conversion training is almost complete. I have already flown observation flights in the Boeing and I am excited to finally get to take my seat in the jet. There is one other formality I must complete in the bureaucratic process. I book an appointment to get my Irish medical issued. Everything is starting to fall into place.

A week later, I am lying down on an examination table at the IAA medical offices in Dublin. I am wearing a gown and I can hear the faint sound of a fan spinning in the machine I am connected to. Several electrodes have been glued to my head and on various parts of my body. I've never had an EEG before and I have no idea what to expect. The man who attached the electrodes leaves the room and turns out the lights. I am confused. "Ok, this is weird," I think to myself. I hear the needles flick on the machine. "Why has he left, am I supposed to do something?" The needles rapidly flick again, like a seismograph recording an earthquake. "Oh shit, it's measuring my brain waves!" Flick, flick, scribble. "Just stop thinking." Scribble, flick. I try to blank out my thoughts.

It seems like five minutes have passed before the door to the room opens abruptly. The light from the corridor shines in and then it is dark again as the door closes. I hear a person walk to the foot of the table and stop. "Bang!" He kicks the bed hard and I jump. The machine goes crazy. He walks to another part of the room. I do not look up to see the man and I am trying my best to stay calm and breathe normally. An old-fashioned telephone rings and the man begins a one-sided conversation. "Oh, hello, it's so great to hear from you after so many years, I really missed you." I play along and start thinking happy thoughts. The machine scribbles. His voice then changes tone. "He's what, oh no, he's dead?" Now I think about sadness and misery. I try to suppress any thoughts about the sheer absurdity of what is happening and I pray that I do not burst out in laughter.

The room is quiet again. I see something approach my head. I stay still. The needles move again. A powerful strobe light flashes at various frequencies right in front of my eyes. It's an awful experience but I try to stay calm. My eyes are literally streaming with tears. This is a test for epilepsy, one I wish they had told me about first. After finishing with the EEG, I go for a hearing test, a chest X-ray, blood test, urine test, treadmill test, eye test and then stand naked in front of three doctors who make a whole host of notes. I wonder if I accidentally walked into astronaut training by mistake! It is near the end of the day and I am sitting opposite the lady who conducted my eye test earlier. "When did you have the laser treatment," she asks. "Over a year ago," I say. "It's healed really well and your vision is perfect, but..."

I am still in shock and only half listening to the words coming from the Head of the Irish Aeromedical Division. I ask my question again. "So, I met and surpassed all the eye tests and you can confirm that I have perfect vision, right?" He seems embarrassed to repeat his answer but he says that he is unable to issue me with an Irish medical certificate despite my perfect score. I just don't know how to respond. This whole day has been ludicrous from the start and now this news makes absolutely no sense. He reaches for a heavy book on the shelf behind him and drops it onto his desk. I look up. "Look, these are the old rules," he says. "Lots of words and lots of room for interpretation." He then places a thin, glossy looking document on top of it. "These are our new rules, blame the bloody Europeans." The document is from the newly formed Joint Aviation Authority (JAA). The JAA is a first attempt at harmonizing all the European aviation authorities and the medical regulations are the first to be implemented. This brand-new document has just become the new law. "There is simply nothing in here allowing you to pass the test by having laser corrective eye surgery, so I can't issue the medical." He doesn't agree with the ruling and knows it is illogical, so he offers to help me. We both know that amending European regulations will take an enormous amount of time and effort but he starts the process by writing to the JAA regulators.

The reality of the situation hits me extremely hard. I will not be walking out with my medical today and my future is very bleak. I have no job, high debts and no career and it's because of the thing I hate the most, bureaucracy. What did I do wrong? Who did I piss off? Why is this happening to me? I really wish that I had got my medical months ago instead of waiting. I leave the building and walk alone next to the River Liffey. It is a very nice day in Dublin. I remove my suit jacket and roll up my sleeves. I stop to watch some birds fly around as a few children feed them breadcrumbs. I find a step and sit down. I have no idea what to do or where to go. My life and dreams have come to a dead end at this place. I begin to organize my thoughts. First, I'll let Les know that I will need some time to fix this issue. Then I'll call the credit card companies and arrange smaller payments. I'll have to accept the extra fees I know I will incur. I need to get a job, and quickly.

I think about my childhood hero, Group Captain Douglas Bader. I begin to understand how he may have felt when bureaucracy stopped his flying career. Douglas had both of his legs amputated after an aircraft accident in the 1930s. He received artificial legs, learned to walk again and flew a perfect test flight with the RAF. However, the medical division denied his application because "there is nothing in the regulations that covers your situation." It would take the start of the Second World War and a shortage of qualified pilots to get the ruling reversed for Douglas. As a fighter pilot, he became an "ace" and flew both the Spitfire and Hurricane during the Battle of Britain. Douglas was taken prisoner in France but managed to escape several times, despite his lack of legs! After the war, Douglas was knighted in recognition of the work he did with children who had lost limbs. His story is one of determination against illogical regulations. The movie made about his life "Reach for the Sky" is my favorite movie of all time. "The rules are written for the obedience of fools and the guidance of wise men," he would say. It seems very appropriate to me right now.

I stand up and begin to walk by the river again. Just like Douglas Bader, I feel the frustration of the irrational rules that appear to have grounded me, despite having met the standards they set. The American FAA didn't hesitate to issue me their highest level of medical certificate, so why do the Europeans take such a different approach? And then it hits me, "of course!" I realize that I do have a valid commercial license from the FAA. Perhaps, I can still fly and be paid if I can find aircraft based in Europe that are registered with the FAA. At least I can still fly while I wait for the authorities to amend the regulations. I have no idea how many aircraft might be available for me to fly within Europe but I am determined to go out and track down any that might exist.

When I return to England, I begin to search for aircraft I can fly. I also learn that some forward thinkers at the CAA are interested in using my case to amend the regulations at the JAA. I am positive again and head out to begin my first day as a freelance FAA commercial pilot in Europe.

FREELANCE PILOT

I am making another "cold-call," trying to sell some computer hardware to a retailer. My success rate for sales is around 30%, which I'm quite happy with and so is my boss, Robin. In fact, he gave me a small personal computer as a "thank you" bonus last week. Robin owns a small Cessna 182 at Old Sarum and he loves to fly. We fly together often, just for fun, and I enjoy showing Robin some basic instrument flying skills. I am twenty-five years old and my quest to find flying work is in full swing. The computer Robin gave me is proving to be very useful. The telephone line I use is slow but I do have access to the Internet, which is relatively new. Many larger companies do not yet have websites of their own but the chance to advertise my pilot services to a European audience is an obvious opportunity I must take. It is free to build a basic website and I have spent many evenings teaching myself basic web design. I slowly create a sharp website to advertise my services as a freelance pilot.

In addition to working for Robin, I also work at Old Sarum airfield doing various jobs for the owner Lesley. Once again, I barely make enough money to pay my rent but this time I have a guardian angel. The airfield accountant, Pam, brings me food parcels every now and then, although I suspect she doesn't realize just how much I rely on her generosity. I have become quite skinny and she jokes that she will stop bringing the parcels when I get my proper ass back! It is raining outside so there is no flying going on today. I am taking a lunch break at one of the restaurant tables inside the flying school, having a cup of coffee with a few other pilots. We are all about the same age and we are feeding off each other, elevating our status as "ace" pilots. We believe we are the top dogs at this airfield and we certainly have the egos to prove it. An older gentleman sits in the corner of the room, quietly listening to our silly banter and conversation. During a lull in our chat, somebody asks him if he was ever an airline pilot. Bill Goldfinch is in his mid-eighties. "Oh no, I never did anything like that." We continue to talk about the large jets we all expect to fly until Bill says, "I did fly in the Royal Air Force when I was younger." Our collective interest is raised. "I flew the Shorts Sunderland," he says.

The others are only slightly interested but I am very impressed. The Sunderland is the military version of the Shorts Sandringham, the huge flying boat I first saw in the Southampton museum. This man flew that wonderful machine, he had the job I dreamed about having all those years ago. As Bill talks, I quickly realize exactly who the top dog in the room really is. Bill explains that he piloted the Sunderland on a rescue mission behind enemy lines during the War. It crashed, killing many on board but he survived and was taken prisoner by the Germans. He escaped so many times that he was finally sent to Colditz, where Douglas Bader was held. In a most audacious plan, Bill designed and helped build a glider he planned to use for an escape over the castle walls and to freedom. The glider was built right under the nose of his captors behind a false wall in an attic using materials acquired from the prison.

Now everyone in the room is listening to his story, and we are all hanging on his every word. With the rain still pounding the window outside, Bill takes a salt & pepper shaker and some cutlery. He takes care to lay them out in a certain way on the table in front of us. He slowly recreates the courtyard layout of Colditz and shows us how he planned to escape. I am absolutely captivated. Bill says that the glider was almost finished but it never flew; the war ended just before the escape was due to be made and he never saw the glider again. Bill Goldfinch is one of the most amazing people I have ever met, a true hero and we become good friends. Listening to this humble man's story, I realize just how little I know and just how little aviation experience I have. The ink on my commercial pilot's license has hardly dried but I have been parading around like I'm Chuck Yeager. I learn a valuable lesson and my ego takes a rightful battering.

A few days later, Robin asks me to take his Cessna to be serviced. I fly to the dealership at Oxford Airport, a familiar destination for me and one where I enjoy the company of the Cessna sales team. Cessna is a very popular brand of private aircraft and the people at Oxford sell their aircraft all over Europe. As I look along the line of new Cessna's sitting on the ramp, something catches my eye; they are FAA registered. These Cessna's are built in America and flown to Oxford and almost all are still carrying their original FAA registration markings. The registration will be changed once each aircraft is sold but until that happens they remain on the FAA register. That means I can fly them! I speak to one of the sales guys, Dustin. He's been looking for an FAA licensed commercial pilot to demonstrate these aircraft to potential buyers. It's a stroke of luck, one of those "right place, right time" events. I'm qualified, licensed and available! With a handshake, I find my first paying job as a freelance pilot.

Within a few weeks, another new American manufacturer in a similar predicament asks for my help. Every weekend, I take a new Cessna or Cirrus to airfields around England and give demonstration flights to potential purchasers. I show the strong points and limitations of the aircraft. Sometimes, I will demonstrate a Cessna on Saturday and return with a Cirrus on Sunday. The money is not great but I am flying and it is a lot of fun sharing these modern machines with other pilots. Both manufacturers pay me a small commission for sales gained following a demo flight.

Cessna is the first to ask me to deliver a recently sold aircraft overseas to an owner in Greece. I am leaving this morning. Finally, I am being paid to fly "international," albeit in a four-seat training aircraft, on my own, and at speeds equivalent to the cars driving below me! It is a crisp morning in the south of England and the Cessna climbs well towards the English Channel. It takes me an hour to fly over the water and reach the French coast. After a couple of short fuel stops, I continue heading south through France and over Monaco before a short flight across the Ligurian Sea leads me to the beautiful French island of Corsica. I decide to spend the night in a cheap hotel on Corsica before completing the delivery tomorrow. "This is the life, the life of a freelance pilot." The hotel in Corsica is older and in need of repair but the air is warm and the stars are shining bright through the large windows in the room. I leave them open and accept a few insects joining me for the night. I just don't care, I want to enjoy all that this new land is offering before I fall asleep. As I lie back on the bed, I feel as if I am on the other side of the planet, millions of miles away from the damp and miserable room in England. I sleep very well.

The remainder of the delivery goes by without a hitch and the following afternoon I am in the warm and sticky climate of Greece. This trip has gone by far too quickly for my liking. I have loved every minute of the 1,500-mile flight and the new owner is happy as I hand over the keys. I get a taxi to the airport and board a commercial flight back to England. I get a window seat and stare down at the passing landscape as it changes from dust to mountains and then to green fields. We fly almost the exact route I flew, just in reverse. Even at 36,000 feet, I manage to glimpse Corsica and I even see the runway I landed on the yesterday evening. I'd do anything to be flying that Cessna through Europe again and I wonder how long it will be before I can do another delivery flight. The next day, my phone rings. It is the people at Cessna bringing some good news about another delivery they want me to complete. Within a couple of months, I am flying new Cessna's to Spain, Italy, Ireland, France, and all over Europe. A smile of contentment follows me to every new country.

During one of my weekend demonstration stops, I see a pretty twin engine Beech Baron sitting on the ramp with its FAA registration markings showing. It doesn't take long to track down the owner and I arrive in his office with a proposal. Ronan has been using the Baron to fly to a few business meetings around England but he is not yet qualified to fly in cloud and so he can only use the Baron on good weather days. He says he is thinking about selling it. I give him a short sales pitch and emphasize the convenience of using the Baron to fly to his offices in Germany instead of flying with the airlines and having to rely on an airline schedule. As a qualified instructor, I can also teach him to fly in cloud whenever we fly together. He nods and smiles, liking what he is hearing. The next week, we fly to Nuremburg. The flight is easy, enjoyable and a great success. Ronan fills my schedule with more flights to his various European offices. It's another lucky break, another way to keep flying and a very enjoyable addition to my other flying work.

It is Mother's Day. Ronan has arranged a surprise flight for his mother. I will fly them to have lunch at a nice restaurant on one of the Channel Islands off the French coast. The table is booked, flowers will arrive during lunch and it is forecast to be a lovely day. I wake up before my alarm sounds. I look at my bedside clock. "Oh crap, no, not today." It is flashing "12:00" The power must have gone out during the night. I pick up my watch, dreading to see what time it is as I need to be at the airport by noon. I'm horrified when I see that it is 11:40am. I tear out of bed and throw on yesterday's clothes. I run to my car, forgetting to lock the front door, while all the time screaming obscenities to myself. This is literally the worst day for this to happen. I have far too many things racing around my mind as I drive as fast as I can towards the airfield. I am not concentrating and at a red light I bang into the back of another car; it's totally my fault. The other driver is fine and there is not too much damage, but I realize I am in no shape to fly and I am going to have to let Ronan and his mother down. I call Ronan's secretary to confess. I can hear Ronan in the background, he is understandably furious. I feel so embarrassed and decide to always set two separate alarms from this day forward.

Through word of mouth, I have been asked to fly another Baron, a slightly larger BE58. I am flying some musicians to France today. It is chilly as I stand with my friend Dave next to the sharp blue and white Baron at a local airfield. I am shocked when I see the band arrive, complete with a ton of equipment. Four larger men, plus bags, plus a keyboard, and a bass guitar and another guitar! The little six-seat Baron does not have enough room for all of this. Eugene, the bandleader, looks at the Baron and quickly comes to the same conclusion. "I thought we had a bigger plane," he says in his smooth Texas accent. They all start laughing. "Well, let's give it a go," I say. First, I put the bags and guitar into the small storage area in the nose of the plane. The bags go in easily but the guitar is slightly too big. I start banging and pushing on the case, trying to force the guitar into the small space. Eugene rushes over. "You know that guitar was played by BB King, right?" I continue a little more carefully. Next, the four members of the band get into the back of the Baron. Two seats face forward and two face backwards. I put the bass guitar across the laps of the first two seats and the keyboard splits the four men in half, with their shoulders taking the weight. There is constant laughter as I welcome the band to their "rock star" transportation. I wish I had a camera to capture the hysteria!

Spirits are high for the three-hour flight to Bordeaux. Eugene has invited us to the concert tonight. It's a very cool setting with an outdoor stage and hay bales for the audience to sit on. The concert begins with a group of French school children destroying some jazz classics. It's a terrible noise but the audience is sympathetic. After a couple of hours, it is Eugene's turn. He and his band are headlining. He whispers in my ear "I'll soon liven the place up." Never have truer words been spoken. Eugene 'Hideaway' Bridges and his band put on a magnificent concert. If I close my eyes, I would swear that Sam Cooke is singing with BB King playing the guitar. The audience responds with loud cheers and everybody is dancing. We are having a great time with Eugene but I remind the band that there is no room for groupies in the Baron! The return flight is equally as entertaining and I suggest that they insist on booking a larger aircraft for their next gig!

Another source of flying work comes from a horse stable. I fly jockeys and trainers to various races in England, Ireland and France. Today, I am flying a group of Irish jockeys from England to Toussus le Noble, near Paris. But there is a problem as I turn onto the runway for takeoff. Before a race, jockeys have a habit of chain smoking to control their weight. The smoke is so thick that I cannot see a thing out of the front window! I have already opened the small ventilation hatch next to me but it's a complete fog inside the eight-seat Piper Navajo. I look back but I can barely see my passengers for the reduced visibility. Three of the jockeys are in full smoke mode. I ask one of the trainers if they can hold their smoking for a couple of minutes to allow me to takeoff. "Feck off, just fly!" I think for a second, I have a sneaky idea. I call back to one of the trainers. "I have a light up here, showing that the back door is still open, can you check it for me?" He goes back and opens the large entry door before slamming it shut. "How's that," he asks. "Almost, try again." He opens and closes the door three times. It's enough to clear most of the smoke. "That's it," I say and I don't hesitate to get airborne before the haze returns. After takeoff, I turn the vents to full blast to keep the "weight loss" smog to a minimum. As we cruise along towards the racetrack, I can't help but remind myself of the "glamourous" job I have.

The freelance work is sporadic but I can cover the cost of my bills. One request from my website will change everything. "I need a ferry pilot, are you available?" I agree but I am not exactly sure what is expected of a ferry pilot.

Within six months, I will become one of the busiest full-time ferry pilots in the world.

Trying to stay warm in a Cirrus SR22 over the North Atlantic.

PART TWO

NOMAD

Ferry Flying

*"I never planned to be a ferry pilot;
well, nobody in their right mind ever would."*

GREEN EGGS

Yakovlev Yak 18T
Lithuania, Poland, Germany, Netherlands, England
(1,060nm 15.1 flying hours)

"It is an absolutely absurd scene. I am still questioning my sanity as I line up at the end of a rough dirt road in the middle of Lithuania ready to fly this untested Russian aircraft. Halfway down the makeshift runway, two men have stopped traffic on the highway that crosses my track. Sitting in the co-pilot seat is a man I have just met, Aleksej, or Alex as he prefers to be called. I have agreed to take him to help translate the Russian words placarded next to the many switches and dials on the cluttered brown instrument panel. Everyone is waiting for me. Alex stares out of the side window as I open the throttle and release the brakes. The thundering engine noise echoes off the factory buildings passing just a few feet either side of this large red machine. With a choking cloud of dust and stones following behind, my first contracted ferry flight has just begun."

One week earlier: Richard hands me an airline ticket. I will leave from Heathrow tomorrow and land in Vilnius, the capital of the former Soviet Republic of Lithuania. This delivery is the first ferrying request I received through my website and Richard, a respected dental surgeon, is giddy with excitement as he talks me through some of the arrangements he has already made. I will be met in

Vilnius by a man called Viktor, who will take me to my hotel and give me the Russian permit authorizing me to fly the unusual machine back to England. After resting at the hotel, I will catch a bus to collect the plane. The four seat Yak-18T is currently in Kaunas, some 70 miles northwest of Vilnius. Richard is trying hard to contain his delight as he shakes my hand and wishes me luck. Later that evening, I sit at my desk and complete a basic plan for the delivery route. There is one annoying issue, the German authorities have denied authorization for me to fly in their airspace because of strict noise regulations. Apparently, the old Yak, with its large radial engine, does not meet their "fly quiet" rules. Flying across northern Germany would be the most direct path but I am forced to plan a longer route, north through Poland, Denmark and Holland before crossing the North Sea to England. It will be a pretty route and so I'm not too concerned.

Heathrow is busy this morning but I arrive at the Lithuanian Airlines gate early. A stressed gate agent hands me a scrap of paper with a seat number written on it. My inquisitive look asks the question and she answers. Apparently, our aircraft has a mechanical issue and so a replacement is being sent with a different seating arrangement, thus requiring the unconventional boarding pass. The delay is not too bad and soon I board a small bus with around fifty other passengers. We are driven out to a remote area of the airport. A silence of disbelief falls over us as the bus stops beside our carriage to Lithuania. The ancient and battered museum piece is a paint faded, hail damaged, three-engine Russian jet airliner. I stare, open-mouthed as a set of rusty rear stairs is lowered from the back of the old aircraft. The same gate agent ushers us up the creaking steps and into the contraption. Inside the cabin, the walls are decorated with a mix of dark brown and cigarette yellow, which compliments a faded green carpet so worn that some of the metal floor is visible beneath it. My thin metal edged seat looks like it has been removed from a 1950's school bus and the seat belt takes several attempts before it locks. Perhaps I should take another flight? Before any of us can change our minds, the largest of the three large flight attendants closes the rear door and a worrying fog of black smoke surrounds us as the tired engines come to life. The cabin is silent as we taxi out, take off, and slowly climb into the English afternoon sky.

It is early evening when we land in Vilnius. After clearing customs, I walk into the elaborately decorated terminal and marvel at some of the sculptures of Russian aviators. A man dressed in a black overcoat and hat is holding a sign with my name on it. This must be Viktor. He acknowledges me with a nod and we walk to his black car outside. I sit on the rear bench seat; there are no seat belts. Viktor lights a cigarette and an older plump woman gets into the car and sits next to me. "Hello," I say. She stares forward and says nothing. I assume that she doesn't speak English. As he starts the car, Viktor tells me that the hotels are full and so I will be staying with him tonight. Coughing loudly from his own cigarette smoke, he speeds through the dreary streets like a Formula One driver. My ever-silent seat companion slides from side to side with each turn until we screech to a stop in an area surrounded by old high-rise buildings. The aloof woman exits the car and walks off into the darkness. Puzzled, I ask Viktor who this silent lady was. "She always wanted to meet someone from England," he says!

I follow Viktor into one of the buildings. The concrete walls of the dark lobby are damp and covered in colorful graffiti. The elevator is broken and so we climb several flights of stairs to reach Viktor's place. His wife, who also doesn't speak English, is waiting for us in the kitchen. Two surprises are waiting for me. First, Viktor insists I dress in a full Lithuanian military uniform and then he takes my photo. It will be added to his unusual guest book once developed! Second, his wife has cooked a "traditional" English dinner for us tonight. This sounds great as I am hungry after my journey. I take my place at the kitchen table but I am horrified when I see the plate in front of me. I simply don't know how to react. I stare at the lime green eggs, black bacon and strange yellow paste swimming in grease on the well-used brown edged plate. I look at Viktor and his wife; they both smile and nod. Before I can respond, they pour some tea, but the tealeaves stay in the mix and float around in the cup. Viktor and his wife stand over me, ever smiling, waiting for me to start eating.

I delay. I tell them the story of my bizarre journey to Lithuania. Only Viktor understands my English but he doesn't translate for his wife. Despite this, she keeps nodding and smiling. I describe our bouncy landing and the few passengers that were still standing in the aisle as we hit the runway. Desperately, I glance around the small kitchen for artifacts that might stimulate some more delaying conversation. What I see brings home an embarrassing truth. It is obvious that Viktor and his wife are living in poverty. The meal that they have prepared for me is a very gracious and generous display of hospitality for a visitor from a foreign land. Ashamed at my own snobbery I clear the plate, smiling back as I eat. Afterwards, I lay on the cool concrete floor with a rough blanket over me waiting for my stomach to complain, but it never does.

I sleep surprisingly well and I am soon shaking Viktor's hand with gratitude as I board a small eight-seat bus, bound for Kaunas. The journey is pleasant but I rarely notice any people working in the endless fields passing by my window. I am dropped off at my destination and the bus leaves. I am met by a man whose name I will never know. He takes me inside a building where I get to see the large red Yak-18T for the first time. Standing around 12 feet tall, 28 feet long with a wingspan of 35 feet it's an impressive aircraft with a huge paddle propeller attached to a large five-cylinder radial engine. The name 'Masha', a Russian diminutive of Maria, is painted on the side in white script. This Yak was originally built to train Aeroflot pilots in Russia. I am introduced to Alex who proudly informs me that they finished the restoration of the Yak earlier today, "right on schedule." This prompts my first question, "who will be flying the test flight?" Alex motions me to hand him my Russian flying permit. He highlights a word with his finger bashing. The word looks like "obnet" but I have no idea what it means. He translates for me. This permit authorizes me to ferry the aircraft to England AND complete the test flight! "I'm not a test pilot," I tell Alex. He shrugs his shoulders and walks off to light another cigarette.

My unexpected test pilot duties are soon plunged into insignificance when I learn about the lack of a runway. My thoughts numb as Alex points to the narrow dirt track he expects me to use for my takeoff. I need a moment and excuse myself, deciding to walk alone along the dirt road to consider my options. It has taken me two days to get here and my choices are very clear. If I do not fly the

89

Yak, somebody else will have to travel here and do it instead. If I refuse this delivery, it will probably be the last contract I'll get. I begin to wonder if I can safely fly off the dirt track. It seems long enough and there appears to be enough space between the buildings. I make my decision. If the performance charts show that I have a safe distance available for the take-off, I'll go. I begin to pace out the dusty track to establish its length. There is a public highway crossing the makeshift runway before a line of small trees marks the end of the track. I briefly consider using the public road as a runway but the closely spaced light posts do not allow enough clearance for the wingtips. I go back and look at the aircraft manual, Alex helps me to translate some of the writing. The numbers seem to work, but there is no margin for error. I must ensure that no cars will be crossing the road as I depart. Following a brief conversation, Alex climbs aboard as my unplanned translator and new co-pilot for the journey across Europe. I begin the antiquated start procedure, shout "clear" from the window and push the large start button.

It's now or never. I look across at Alex but he looks completely bored. The gravely path ahead is clear and so I take a breath and push the large brown throttle lever fully forward. There is a gray blur where the propeller blades were wind milling a second ago. Everything in the aircraft shakes violently as we gather speed along the dirt track. The trees at the far end are closing rapidly as we careen towards the stopped cars on the road. Some of the drivers are standing next to their cars, watching and smoking their cigarettes as if this is a regular occurrence. The needle on the jarring airspeed indicator moves towards a lime green number, 130 kilometers per hour, the speed I have determine to be safe for takeoff. I heave back on the large control wheel and we flounder into the air barely missing the tops of the trees. I look back over my left shoulder and feel terrible for the co-operative drivers whose cars I have just showered with dirt and rocks. The noise from the engine is deafening, like a continuous thunderstorm cracking inches in front of me. I understand why Germany decided to ban me from using their airspace but I soon settle into the trembling office and go through some of the required test maneuvers. Despite the noise, vibration and unconventional controls, the Yak is flying very well. I easily determine that 'Masha' is fully airworthy and safe to complete the journey ahead. Alex and I begin to chat, but he keeps his devious plan from me, for now.

After almost three hours of flying and with dusk arriving, the noise and vibration of this surprisingly comfortable aircraft have become familiar to us. We are flying over Poland and I am setting up for an approach to Gdansk Airport where Alex and I will spend the night. Below us is the famous Gdansk Shipyards, the birthplace of the Solidarity movement. This resilient movement led by Lech Walesa, resulted in the fall of Communist Party rule in Poland during the late 1980's. For his part, Mr. Walesa was awarded the Nobel Peace Prize and eventually became the president of Poland. I make another turn towards the long asphalt runway and gaze at the large shipyard cranes coming into view on my left. A light mist is flowing in from the inlet and the scene is reminiscent of the images I saw on television news when I was growing up. I can imagine the tens of thousands of Polish workers gathering to listen to their leader as they prepared to change history. After a relatively smooth landing, I taxi Masha to the overnight parking area and I catch sight of the sign on the terminal building, *Gdansk Lech Walesa Airport*. I am struck that one man was able to inspire an entire country into choosing a different path for its future and I am keen to explore his town.

Alex and I are suitably pleased to have successfully completed the first day of our delivery and we are looking forward to sampling some Polish hospitality. The old town of Gdansk, sitting on the banks of the Mollawa River, is nothing short of spectacular as we walk past line after line of colorful old buildings. I really feel as if I have traveled back in time as I look up at the fascinating flamboyant buildings that ooze with almost 1,000 years of rich history. We sit down in one of these low ceiling buildings and try some traditional pierogi. It's the first time I have tried it, and at first it sounds comparable to those green eggs. However, the hot dough pockets filled with cheese, cabbage, pork, mushrooms and potatoes are delicious and pair very well with a few jars of local beer. After satisfying our hunger, we walk along the stone streets back to the guest house and I glide into a satisfying sleep.

The weather is co-operative the next morning and we have no issues leaving Gdansk. However, fifteen minutes after takeoff something catches my eye on the instrument panel. A little needle is pointing to a number "3" on a small gauge that I suspect is our oil temperature indication. Worryingly, number "3" is deep in the red painted markings but everything else seems fine. The engine is still shaking and rattling in the same way that it did yesterday and I ask Alex if he knows what the gauge might be indicating. He doesn't; it's a gauge without a placard. I begin a process of elimination, checking all the other gauges and seeing how they react when I reduce and increase power. Soon, I am convinced that this gauge is our engine oil temperature indication. I believe that the "3" is 300 degrees Celsius, which would justify a hot indication. The oil pressure gauge is normal and the suspect gauge never moves when I change power settings, so I believe it is faulty.

We are about to head over the Baltic Sea towards Denmark and so, to be safe, I decide to alter the route and stay over land until I can be sure that the gauge is the true problem. I grab my map and begin a rough re-route using my "10nm" thumb to approximate my new flying time. Conveniently, when I bend my thumb, the length matches exactly the equivalent of 10 nautical miles on many aviation maps. I lay my thumb down on the map and count, 10nm, 20nm, 30nm, 40nm, Germany! The coastal route will mean entering German airspace 50nm from here, about 20 minutes of flying time. I wonder if I should return to Gdansk but I don't belive I have anything to lose by asking. I call the German controller and request permission to enter his airspace. I explain my predicament and assure him that earplugs will not be necessary as I will fly off the coast but within gliding distance of land in the event the engine decides to quit. He is surprisingly accommodating and issues a clearance. I move the large control wheel and set course towards the coastline. Unknowingly, I am flying towards one of the most extraordinary sights I will ever see.

We are flying along the coast at 3,000 feet about half a mile from the German coast. Ahead of us, there is a point of land covered with beautiful pine trees and a gorgeous half-moon crescent sandy beach. The engine is still running well and I feel relaxed. Something in the trees catches my attention but I can't figure out what it is. It looks like a very long and large gray slab, cut into the forest about

200 feet back from the beach. The slab seems to stretch into the distance for over a mile. I am puzzled by the sight. Why would somebody put a long line of concrete into a gorgeous natural pine forest? As we fly closer, I can see that the slab is an incredibly long building, several stories high. There doesn't seem to be anyone working in the colossal structure and it appears to have been abandoned a long time ago. I fly a little lower to get a better look. Most of the windows frames are rusted and there are only a few that still have glass. I simply cannot fathom the sight I am seeing and so I ask the air traffic controller to tell us about it.

This is *Prora*. The faulty oil temperature needle has inadvertently brought Alex and I to one of the longest buildings in the world and a relic of Nazi propaganda. What I first saw as a slab in the trees is in fact a 3-mile long concrete building rising 7 stories high. The original plan was to make *Prora* a holiday retreat for the hardest working socialist workers. Construction was begun in the late 1930s by National Socialist Party workers who wanted to promote the benefits of socialism to the rest of the world. To be sure that people took notice, the building had to be gigantic so that it could never be ignored. The building project was named *Strength Through Joy* but it was never completed. World War Two broke out near the end of construction and so the 9,000 builders were relocated to fight for Adolf Hitler, a man whose destructive objectives couldn't be more contrasting to those of Lech Walesa. Flying the length of *Prora* is a spectacle I know will be hard to forget. As we reach the end of the building, I look back over my shoulder to get one last glimpse before turning Masha towards Maribo, on the southern tip of Denmark.

Our brief stop in Denmark allows time to refuel the big red Yak and to have the faulty oil temperature gauge repaired. I know the gauge is broken as it still reads "3" when I shut the engine down. However, it is a required instrument for flight and so it must work before we get airborne. However, I receive some bad news. There is nobody at the airfield available to fix the gauge today and so we are grounded, which irritates me as we have only flown for a few hours. I begin tapping away at the silly gauge, something pilots seem to do when annoyed and something that never seems to change anything. As I tap the gauge, the needle suddenly releases itself and springs back to its correct position. I start the engine and perform several tests, trying to get the needle to stick again, but it doesn't. We are good to go!

As we taxi out, I am very happy to be back on schedule but a little disappointed that I won't get to explore the beautiful town on the shores of Lake Maribo. All I have is a small leaflet to learn about the history of Maribo. "Saint Birgitta established Maribo after ordering her monks to form a cloister in the early 1300's. The town coat of arms shows Saint Birgitta standing among the clouds." The description of the historic buildings in the area teased my curiosity and I am sad not to be exploring instead of flying. However, Richard is expecting his Yak to turn up tomorrow afternoon and so my thoughts turn back to the job at hand. We are flying towards Holland, where we will stop for the night. An unpleasant surprise is waiting for us.

"So, you don't have your passport with you?" The immigration people in Holland are the first to ask for our passports since we left Lithuania. I have mine but Alex checks his pockets and confirms that he doesn't have it with him. I explain that we left in a rush but the two uniformed officers are not impressed. I tell them that our Yak is not suitably equipped for night flying and so, one way or another, we will have to spend the night in Holland. Nonchalantly, they motion Alex towards the police car for a ride to the local jail! Alex goes crazy. The officers try to calm him down. They reiterate to Alex that he is not under arrest but the jail is "simply a comfortable place to stay tonight." Alex begins to settle down when they promise not to lock the cell door. I feel terrible for Alex, who seems less than enthusiastic about spending a night behind bars, locked or not. I ask the officers to let us stay at the airport hotel and I promise we will confine ourselves to our rooms. It is late, we are tired and there is nowhere else for us to go. I promise that we will leave first thing in the morning and I agree to take full responsibility for Alex. The officers discuss this new proposal and agree. Thankful, we walk to the hotel and I say goodnight to Alex as he closes the wooden door on his room across the hallway. I can't help but think about the chilling noise the iron bars in the local jail would have made if the officers hadn't been so accommodating.

I wake in a sweat at 3am. The troubling predicament is clear to me. Leaving Holland in a few hours will satisfy our agreement with the Dutch immigration officers but what about when we reach England? As the captain of the aircraft, I am responsible for everything on board my aircraft, including Alex. I shudder to think about the consequences for knowingly transporting an undocumented person into the country. Sitting in an English prison will be a bad way to end my first delivery flight. I hastily dress and knock on Alex's door. I ask him to take a flight back to Lithuania in the morning. However, Alex has already realized the same issue and has been working on a solution. He just contacted a friend in Kaunas who agreed to fax copies of his documents to the immigration people in England. He says that his friend will make the necessary arrangements in the morning as we fly. I am worried that he will be detained while they wait for the documents to arrive but Alex says he is happy to take the risk. I am a little uncomfortable but I agree.

My alarm wakes me a few hours later and I meet Alex for breakfast. We are surprised when the same two immigration officers meet us for chocolate croissants and coffee. They are friendly and even offer to pay the bill. The familiar cloud of oily smoke wafts around us as the large radial engine splutters to life for our last day of flying. As we settle into the cruise, I check the oil temperature gauge, which is now functioning normally. I relax into my seat for our North Sea crossing towards England. It is a gorgeous day. The sun is blazing down from above and the tall flare stacks on the oil rigs below are bright as they burn off excess gas from their pressure relief systems. The pressure of completing this delivery is also released a little as I settle the red Yak onto a long asphalt runway in the southeast of England. We have one more leg to fly before this delivery is complete and I am keen to get going. All we must do here is clear customs, immigration and refuel. However, Alex has gone missing.

A small part of me expected it. Alex lives in Kaunas, a poor industrial area that is dirty and dusty. It is a complete contrast to the lush green fields and clean air of this part of England. I guess that Alex has been planning his escape all along but his decision was probably finalized as we touched down. I will never know as it is the last time I see him. The immigration officer is not too concerned and says she will pass along the message for their officers to lookout for him and she sends me on my way. Unknown to me, Lithuania is preparing to join the European Union, giving Alex and all Lithuanian's the right to live and work in England. I get back into the Yak and start up again wondering if Alex is watching somewhere around the large airfield. He will certainly hear the noisy takeoff and I silently wish him luck as I coax the red Yak into the air for the final time on this delivery.

Flying alone over the south of England, I recall the curious events of the past few days and wonder if this has been a typical ferry flight. I have received a few more delivery requests from my website and so I will soon have the chance to find out. But, this delivery still has one more twist waiting for me when I land. I hand over the keys to Richard, my first smiling ferry flight owner. As we stand on the ramp, a mechanic removes the engine cowling. "Come and see this," he says. He gently pulls at one of the spark plug leads and it comes away in his hand! Richard and I are equally shocked when we see that there is no plug attached at the end of the lead. Further investigation reveals that two more leads are incorrectly installed. In total, three cylinders have been receiving only half of the ignition sparks they should have been getting.

After fixing the leads, I sit next to Richard as he flies Masha for the first time. Now that all the spark plugs are firing correctly, I marvel at how smooth this previously trembling, shaky and wobbly home has become. I chuckle to myself and look over at Richard who is beaming from ear to ear. He is extremely happy with his new aircraft and I stare out of the side window as a torrent of satisfaction flows through me. This is the first hit of what will soon become an addiction; the ferrying drug. I have yet to experience the true dangers of ferry flying but I have thoroughly enjoyed this delivery and I am itching for another.

The red Yak 18 'Masha' after my delivery

HAPPY VALLEY

Cirrus Design SR20
USA, Canada, Ireland, Netherlands
(3,760nm 30.4 flying hours)

"I am in serious trouble and nobody can help me. Fumbling in the darkness, I reach up and remove the small plastic cover in the roof of the small cockpit. The sound of ripping Velcro briefly drains out the drone of the propeller in front of me. I locate the small metal 'T' handle and grip it with my right hand; it is ice cold. Pulling this handle will fire the one-time use emergency aircraft parachute housed in the back of this brand-new Cirrus SR20. I pause for a moment to clear my head and try to determine the right moment to pull. I know that if I survive the crash into the snow-covered mountains, I have almost no chance of being alive by sunrise."

Five months after the Yak delivery: My dreams of becoming a commercial pilot never included the prospect of smashing into the side of a Canadian mountain. I'd become a full-time ferry pilot by accident but I am now one of the busiest pilots on the North Atlantic delivery route. I have learned and seen many of the dangers. I accept that I have almost no chance of surviving an Atlantic ditching if the engine fails during a crossing. To balance the risk, I am always aware of exactly how the engine is performing. I constantly monitor the engine instruments, listening for miniscule changes in RPM and tracking even the slightest change in aircraft speed. Several ferry

101

pilots have already perished since I began full-time deliveries. They were good pilots who accepted the risks of this job. Knowledge and experience help to lessen the dangers but my acceptance of the inherent hazards came after a conversation I had with an experienced ferry pilot a few deliveries back. Simon and I were sipping coffee in Bangor, Maine, while we waited for our ferry tanks to be installed. He told me that one of three things would happen to me if I decided to continue ferry flying for more than one year:

1. *Die*
2. *Join a monastery*
3. *Be committed to a lunatic asylum*

At the time, we both chuckled, but soon after our conversation I heard that Simon had crashed during an approach into Greenland on a bad weather day. The mountain he hit destroyed the small Piper he was ferrying and Simon was killed instantly. I had been lucky with my crossings to this point and his crash was the wake-up I needed and the self-acknowledgement of the dangers that I required to be able to continue. Despite the risks, the work is very addictive. Being paid to fly a multitude of different aircraft and soaking up the stunning views of our Earth from my airborne office is wonderful. I relish the many hours of happy solitude and I love not knowing where my next job will take me.

Tonight, I am delivering a new Cirrus SR20, built in Duluth and bound for Holland. I have delivered several of these wonderful aircraft during the past few months and I love to fly them. The modern cockpit, comfortable leather seats and side-stick controls make this aircraft stand out as one of the best available. The cruising speed is around 150 knots, or 170 mph. This is faster than similar four-seat private aircraft, thanks in part to the larger 200 horsepower engine. I left Duluth several hours ago, heading for my first stop at Goose Bay in eastern Canada. Behind me is a large aluminum fuel tank loaded with the fuel I need to stay airborne for 10 hours tonight. The sun has already set and I am contemplating how to overcome the serious predicament I have found myself in.

The nearest airport is hundreds of miles away, far beyond the range of the standard VHF radio installed in this aircraft. Even if I was in range, I doubt anybody would answer my call and there isn't much they could do for me anyway. It is 1am, during the middle of winter in the middle of arctic Canada. I am at 9,000 feet, flying alone. Every few seconds, the pitch-black outside is interrupted by a short bright flash from the wing strobe lights. Each flash momentarily exposes the ocean of ice-cold droplets that I am flying through. The ice is collecting on my wings at an alarming rate. It is only a matter of time before this increasing mass of ice will disrupt the airflow enough to eliminate all the aerodynamic lift currently keeping me airborne. I turn off the strobes, preferring to mask reality with darkness.

Descending into warmer air might help to stop the ice forming but below me are the Otish Mountains, jagged peaks rising to almost 4,000 feet with enormous sheer cliffs plunging into ice-covered lakes at their base. I wish the mountains would reveal themselves from their disturbing cloak of darkness. In theory, deploying the emergency parachute will allow a vertical impact into the concealed granite below but the half-million-dollar aircraft will almost certainly be destroyed, even if I am able to survive. The other option is to blindly descend into the blackness with the small landing light shining ahead and hope that a suitable landing area comes into view before impact. I decide against this option; it's far too dangerous, especially with that potential bomb sitting just a few inches behind me. I turn and check the heavy straps that are securing the 105-gallon ferry fuel tank, which is still more than half full of highly flammable aviation fuel. Using the parachute to crash-land in an upright position with a more vertical impact is my best option.

If I survive the impact without serious injury, I am less than confident about lasting through the night in the sub-zero temperatures coming from the blizzard I am flying through. I have very little space for survival equipment in the small aircraft cabin and what I do have is far more suitable for a water ditching. I know that it will be a very long time before rescuers will turn up. The first that anyone will even know about my crash will be at least 5 hours from now. This is the estimated arrival time I entered onto my flight plan before I left the Cirrus factory in Minnesota. A search will only be triggered if I fail to reach my destination at the scheduled time. Until then, I have no real obligation to communicate with anyone and I haven't for almost one-hour. It will be a challenge for my rescuers to find my last position as the route I planned is almost 1,500 miles long and it will take time for them to calculate where to start looking. I resign myself to the truth, that nobody will even know I am missing until tomorrow. I am completely on my own if I am to survive this one. If I could only transmit my position to somebody, at least the rescuers would have an area to start their search. It could make all the difference.

Picking the best time to pull the handle and deploy the chute requires a constant assessment of my situation. I use my thick gloves to wipe away a patch of frost on the left window and I illuminate the wing with my flashlight. A very thick layer of clear ice has formed, following the exact contour of the wing. I get that "heart sinking" feeling when I see that almost the first third of the wing is completely covered. This is not what I want to see as the extra weight of ice is already slowing my airspeed considerably, making a climb virtually impossible. The Cirrus has a beautiful but aerodynamically critical "laminar flow" wing, which is very efficient but requires an even flow of air to work. Any contamination disrupting the airflow reduces the lifting capability of the wing and if the ice continues to build at this rate, the aircraft will soon become uncontrollable.

At least I am still airborne right now, but I know it can't continue for much longer. Since entering this un-forecast ice storm 15 minutes ago, I have been using full power to overcome the extra weight of the ice and maintain my altitude of 9,000 feet. However, the ice has become too heavy and the engine is demanding my help to maintain a minimum flying speed. I have no idea how far the storm stretches ahead but I know that I need to start descending to gain a few more critical knots of airflow over the wings. I start with a shallow descent at first, 50 feet per minute, before steepening the rate and sacrificing more of the airspace protecting me from those peaks below. I begin humming a tune I've never heard before, gripping the parachute handle and waiting for the right moment to pull it. The turbulence begins to increase as I descend and I struggle to read the jarring instruments in front of me. Despite my dire prospects, I am calm and conscious of everything that is happening to the Cirrus outside my window. I am as focused as I have ever been and I begin to pull on the parachute handle.

I freeze when I hear a faint voice on the radio. It sounds like a Canadian voice, barely readable over the background static. Immediately, the calm leaves me and the noise returns. I let go of the parachute handle. Nothing else matters right now. I must communicate with these people and give them my current position. I transmit my call sign but the adrenalin is shaking my words. I strain to hear the reply of a human voice as I hold the headset hard against my head, trying to drown out some of the wind and engine noise. I hear nothing. I am too far away or too low for them to hear me. I punch down on the empty leather seat next to me in frustration. A climb is out of the question and only luck will determine whether they are flying towards me at a high enough speed to hear my call before I crash. I glance at the altimeter, 6,200 feet and descending.

Every second is becoming more critical than the last. I hear the voice again, a little stronger this time. I broadcast my tail number, position and predicament in as few words as possible, words that can never be misinterpreted. The voice responds, they have heard me! I am elated and filled with a renewed purpose. They read back my position and say they will maintain a listening watch. "Good luck," I hear. I am back in the game. The ice-covered windscreen reflects the glow of the instrument panel and I catch a glimpse of my reflection. Despite my uncertain future, I am smiling. The look in my eyes is unmistakable to me. I pull hard on my seat belts and put my hand back onto the parachute handle. I am determined to survive this impact.

I watch the altimeter gradually wind down towards 4,000 feet. This is the altitude I have decided will be the best to pull the parachute handle. I am angry that there will be no delighted, smiling, owner to meet this Cirrus. Instead, he will be receiving news that his very expensive aircraft was destroyed before he even got to fly it. I imagine him receiving the news, "the ferry pilot has used the safety parachute and destroyed your aircraft before it has even flown its first 100 hours." I mutter a string of obscenities to myself. I am proud of my perfect delivery record but my failure to deliver this Cirrus is about to ruin everything.

Then, something extraordinary happens. It is so unexpected, that I discard it at first. This virtually disabled aircraft, barely generating enough airspeed for flight, accepts my ambitious input to level-off and then climb. My eyes widen but experience makes me cautious. I keep my hand on the parachute handle. But up I go, 50 feet, 100 feet. The turbulence increases considerably, something I know happens near the edge of some storm systems. Perhaps this is the end of the storm? My mind is rapidly assessing, questioning and second-guessing everything I see. Maybe I am so close to the mountaintops that this upward trend is the mountain air pushing up over the peaks. If this is true then the force of the plunging air on the other side will undoubtedly pull me into the rock to a crash that I will not survive.

The incredible jolting turbulence is making it hard for me to focus on the instruments as I search the dials for clues of my fate. I am still climbing, albeit very slowly. My adrenaline surges as a banging sound begins, like large bags of pebbles being thrown at the fuselage. I guess that it must be ice pellets. I wipe the side window with my glove and shine my flashlight onto the wing to assess this latest issue, but I am confused by what I see. I look away and then back again to confirm it. The ice is almost completely gone. And then I realize that there are no ice pellets hitting me, the banging noise is simply small chunks of ice breaking off the wings and striking the fuselage and tail.

I take my hand off the parachute handle and slam the throttle lever hard against the stop, aching to exit this storm. The turbulence is so rough that it threatens to push my overworked wings to breaking point but the battered aircraft climbs ever upwards. The turbulence rises to a crescendo and makes everything inside the small cockpit fly around from side to side. My seat belts strain against my shoulders, but then, with one gut-wrenching crack, the curtain of ice covering the windscreen suddenly slips away uncovering a million bright stars. Immediately, the air is still. I look ahead for a second storm but there's nothing in view but dark and clear skies. I grab my flashlight and check the fuselage for damage. Nothing, all seems fine. I take a breath and wipe the sweat from my forehead. My heart is still pumping hard. I was probably only a few feet from striking the terrain but I am now in the clear. The plastic parachute handle cover is on the floor next to my foot so I loosen my seat belt, reach down and replace it. I close my eyes for a few seconds to reset my balance. My escape is now assured.

I get back to work and look at the chaos left in my cockpit. My position logs and weather charts are scattered around me along with some snacks, water bottles and my large, currently empty, apple juice container. I will need to use this relief container soon. I methodically return some order to my claustrophobic space. Slowly, I ease back into the calm routine of plotting and monitoring. I have missed my last plot entry, something I choose to do every 15 minutes. Keeping track allows an analysis of the engine health and an accuracy check of the charted weather systems. I begin to wonder how I overlooked the storm behind me.

I planned my flight this morning while eating pancakes with my friend Joe at Sara's Table Cafe in Duluth. I always plan my flights meticulously and I hate weather surprises. Perhaps I had missed something while I was enjoying the maple syrup? I look at the charts again but they show nothing but clear air. I decide that it must have been a freak storm, one of those that pop up every now and then as a reminder to avoid complacency. I find my chart, plot my current position using a small "x" and write the current time, outside air temperature, altitude, winds and engine parameters next to it. I then determine my fuel remaining against that required to complete the flight. The storm passage has forced me to use a little extra fuel but I still have enough for the 5 hours remaining before I will see the bright runway lights at Goose Bay Airport.

Most ferry pilots use Goose Bay as a transit point before crossing the North Atlantic. It is perfectly located at the mouth of Lake Melville just a few miles from the shores of the Atlantic Ocean. The airport was built in 1941 in response to the outbreak of World War Two. At one point during the war, Goose Bay was the busiest airport in the world, handling thousands of military aircraft embarking on transatlantic journeys to support the war effort. Today, the airport still has a military presence but it is the small private aircraft flown by ferry pilots that continue the tradition of stopping here before crossing the Atlantic Ocean to Europe.

I fly over the small iron-ore town of Labrador City, 350 miles west of Goose Bay. There is nothing but a barren tundra of snow and ice between the two cities, which is beautiful during clear days but as black as coal tonight. The horizon is clearly defined where the millions of stars end and the solid black of earth begins. As I stare into the darkness something strange happens. At first, I believe my cockpit is being surrounded by smoke. Surely, this is not another storm developing? Then, the lights are switched on to reveal themselves, bright green swirling wisps of charged atoms; the Aurora Borealis. I wonder if Mother Nature is apologizing for her earlier storm as this amazing green light show seems to be playing just for me. Everywhere I gaze, the Northern Lights are pirouetting around me. I recline my seat and stare through the window, dumbfounded by the incredibly beautiful display. Every now and then, highly charged areas shoot upwards into the sky like a firework tail and illuminate everything around me. I am captivated by such an amazing natural show from my privileged front row seat. As I watch, I think of wartime pilots who must have also seen their cockpits light up with the ghostly green as they flew to Goose Bay. At the time, they were facing an uncertain future heading to war, but perhaps they had a similar moment of tranquility as they marveled at such an amazing spectacle.

I am getting ready to land. The sun is cracking over the horizon ahead of me as the welcoming 2-mile long runway at Goose comes into view. The snow-covered runway is particularly slippery this morning and I lock up the brakes momentarily. The exhaustion of this flight is obviously affecting me. Carefully, I guide the brand-new machine towards the parking ramp and shut-down. As the propeller stops, I make my final log entry for this leg. The total flight time from Duluth was 9hrs 14mins, a good test before I cross the Atlantic to Ireland tomorrow. The engine has performed flawlessly, giving me confidence to continue. In the confines of the small cockpit, I twist and stretch to remove my thick yellow rubber survival suit. The outside air temperature gauge reads -35°C. I pull my thick hat down over my ears and cover my face with a scarf to prevent the driving winds from burning my skin. I occasionally slip as I cross the short distance to the warm and inviting Woodward's office. I have seldom been so happy to see Nickki and the smiling FBO girls. I share the story of my close call as they hand me a welcome mug of hot chocolate. Nickki doesn't stay close to me for too long. She knows that a ferry pilot is at his most pungent shortly after removing a several hours old rubber suit! Soon, the van arrives to take me to Linda's B&B, a regular stop for ferry pilots.

In the summer, the incredible beauty of this mostly untouched and vast natural landscape is something many people come to enjoy. Bird watchers turn up to see seven or eight species of visiting geese. Goose Bay is appropriately named in this respect, however, the original name for the local town was the less than enticing *Refugee Cove*. Despite living in a bitter and unforgiving freezer for most of the year, the locals are always so cheerful and so they decided to ditch this name and change it to *Happy Valley* in 1955. During one night at Trappers Bar, I'd charged a local with false advertising of his town, citing the horizontal snow flying past the windows as my evidence. I compared the name Happy Valley to the equally deceptive name given to the snow-covered country of *Green*-Land. How could anyone be happy in this bitterly cold and isolated place? All I got back in return that night was smiles from the residents and offers of more drinks.

The Woodward's van drives past a large wooden sign at the entrance to the town, *Welcome to Happy Valley-Goose Bay*. Despite the regular arctic temperatures and frequent driving snow, the friendly and warm people of Goose Bay epitomize the name of the town that they love. When I think back to the prospect of perishing on an icy mountaintop in the middle of nowhere, I feel very much at home and I smile to myself. I am very happy to be in Happy Valley tonight.

Pumping hot air into the cold Cirrus engine at Goose Bay

SUNNY SLEEP

Beech King Air C90
USA, Russia, Japan
(7,120nm 50.7 flying hours)

"I don't have enough fuel to make Petropavlovsk and the Russians have denied my request to shorten my route. They have threatened military interceptors if I disobey. I turn the transponder switch off and on several times to try and convince the controllers that I have an equipment malfunction. Without the transponder on, I will effectively disappear from their radar screens. After a few more cycles of the switch I leave it off and ease the King Air a few precious degrees to the left. The controller questions my position. I stall for time while I cut the corner of the ridiculously inefficient route. "Let me see if I can reset it." After a few minutes, I rejoin the airway and turn the transponder back on. "You are radar identified," the monotone Russian voice says. I feel smug and then the low fuel light illuminates."

It is one month after the Cirrus flight: I have been using the computer Robin gave me to build a more useful website and to promote my ferrying services instead of just general freelance flying. The websites of most ferry companies are basic and contain little information for a potential client. I have a chance to get ahead and build a good reputation while they all figure out their marketing mistakes. I think of every standard question a client might ask about an aircraft delivery and I try to answer them as accurately and truthfully as I can.

What will it cost to ferry my plane?
How long will it take?
What if there are mechanical problems?
Who insures the flight?
Do I pay up front or at the end?
Is the delivery pilot experienced?

I try to add a little humor and I post photographs of previous aircraft I have delivered. I draw inspiration for the site from Richard Branson and the approach his Virgin company takes. Their strategy seems to be: keep it simple, be honest and turn the small print into the large print. I like this "no surprises" approach and adopt it as best as I can. I get several quote requests as a result but only a handful turn into deliveries, meaning a lot of planning for very little paid flying. I do most of my quotes at my small desk in a moldy basement room that I am now renting in the south of England, near to Stonehenge.

I receive a quote request from a Japanese aircraft broker. They say that their normal delivery pilot has let them down and they need an eight seat, twin-turboprop business plane collected in Iowa and flown to southwestern Japan as soon as possible. This delivery sparks my interest as I love flying the type of aircraft to be delivered, a Beech King Air C90. I sit at my little desk, get my maps out and take a little extra time to ensure that my quote is competitive. By the next morning, I have a signed contract, but there is a twist.

The new owner and his personal pilot want to ride along with me. Honestly, I hate "babysitting" passengers while I am working as I much prefer the freedom to operate on my own timetable and explore towns incognito, quietly blending in and watching the world go by. The broker reassures me that the two passengers will be "no trouble at all" and that many more delivery contracts will find their way to me if I can accommodate. I could use some extra work and perhaps it will be fun? I agree and arrange to meet my passengers in Chicago after I collect the King Air and have the chance to ensure it is ready to cross the Pacific.

A few days later, I land in northern Chicago and meet my passengers, Mr. Nakamura and Mr. Yamashita. They are typical of the Japanese I have met: kind, quiet, respectful, courteous and constantly smoking! Nakamura sits in one of the comfortable leather seats in the back while Yamashita takes a seat up front with me. I call air traffic control and pick up my flight plan clearance to our first stop, Dickinson Airport in North Dakota. We will have a small headwind along the route and so I fly at an altitude that satisfies my requirement for long-range flight with minimal fuel-burn. Speed is not a consideration for me during a delivery flight but fuel economy is at the top of the list. I always fly at a most unhurried rate of knots when I am ferrying. As we inch along the flat agricultural plains below, it doesn't take too long for the boredom to set in for my two passengers.

When designing my website, I asked several people to tell me the biggest concern about having their aircraft delivered. Unexpected costs is often the top answer. To solve this issue, I decided to do things a little differently and began offering all-inclusive delivery quotes. This puts the burden on me to fly efficient routes, utilize winds and plan an intelligent schedule to ensure I stay within budget and make a profit. The owner simply pays one amount and then waits for their aircraft to turn up. The Japanese broker has already paid this "no hassle" price and so the request I receive from my two passengers is quite easy for me to answer. Yamashita joins me in the cockpit. "Perhaps, you fly faster," he says, nodding his head to try and encourage me. Yamashita has been in the back with Nakamura for about 20 minutes and I sensed that they were plotting something. A deflated "ah" is his response as I politely refuse, citing an obligation for me to make a profit and pay my rent.

It's windy and dusty when we land in Dickinson. This will be a quick fuel and coffee stop for us. My two passengers have been discussing something while we have been on the ground. Again, I sense a plan is being drawn up but I pretend not to notice. Soon, we are airborne and I level off at 22,000 feet. The air is smooth and the view ahead is clear. Yamashita joins me again. "Perhaps you fly faster, and Nakamura pay for best hotels and best food on trip?" I pause and think for a second. Maybe a little of the good life will be fun? Yamashita smiles as I push the throttles forward, triggering new life from the two exquisite Pratt and Whitney turboprops. I look back and get a thumbs-up as a celebratory cigarette is duly lit and we fly on at high-speed towards our overnight stop in Seattle.

The scenery below is breathtaking from our small window looking down on the world. We are about an hour from Seattle and Yamashita has joined me in the cockpit. He takes time to ask about the instruments and dials in the well-designed panel. Once we arrive in Japan, the captain's seat will become his. His dry sense of humor is on display. "Oh, too many dials, too complicated!" I smile back as I know he has recently completed his training for the King Air and he is also a very experienced pilot. Yamashita recently retired as a senior Boeing 767 captain for a Japanese airline. He has crossed the Pacific many hundreds of times before but this is his first at such a low level and with so many fuel stops along the way. He tells me that he really enjoyed learning to fly the King Air. I offer him the chance to fly some of the legs on our ferry flight but he prefers to sit back and enjoy the trip instead.

I ask how the two friends first met. Yamashita explains that he met Nakamura at flight school during the 1970s. Until now, I never realized that Nakamura was a pilot too. They became good friends and flew a Japanese built sixty seat commuter airliner together, the YS-11. At some point, Nakamura decided to pursue a business career while Yamashita continued flying. The two had recently reconnected when Nakamura purchased the King Air and needed a pilot. As we chat, Yamashita looks down through the window and says, "Ah, Enola Gay." His comment catches me totally off guard. I am embarrassed at my lack of knowledge as he explains that we are flying over the Hanford Site in Washington State. This is where the plutonium was manufactured for the atomic bombs that were dropped on Japan. His knowledge impresses me. Some 80,000 Japanese people were killed when two bombs were dropped on Nagasaki and Hiroshima, effectively ending World War Two. Yamashita realizes my anxious inability to conjure up any appropriate responses. I just don't know what to say without causing offense. He puts his hand on my shoulder and calmly says, "it's ok, Japanese very, very bad."

I catch sight of Mount Rainier, a huge snow-covered volcano peak to the southeast of Seattle rising to almost 14,000-feet. It is a striking spectacle as we fly past at almost the same level. Nakamura joins us up front to get a better view. "Wow," the three of us say in unison. Just to the left of Mount Rainier are the remains of Mount St. Helens. The top of the peak is missing because of an incredible eruption in 1980, which blew 1,300 feet from the summit. I can remember watching TV news of this spectacular eruption as a young boy but it seemed to be another world away from my monotonous life in the south of England. I certainly never expected that I would be flying over the top of the mile-wide crater several years later. I gaze down with fascination and trace the lava flows that are now solidified after decades of cooling. Nakamura and Yamashita are both smiling. They are enjoying our trip and that matters a great deal to me.

I spread out my various navigation maps on a desk in the swanky Seattle hotel room Nakamura booked for me tonight. Often, the flying is the easiest part of my delivery flights. Airspace entries, over-flight permissions and landing permits are part of a bureaucratic minefield I enter each time I plan a ferry flight. For this flight, I have already received permission to enter eastern Russian airspace. My time window to cross the BAMOK intersection, a Pacific Ocean airspace entry point just to the west of the Aleutian Islands, is set for 2:15pm three days from now. The Russian authorities give a buffer of just +/- 15 minutes, which demands that my flight planning skills are polished. With the increase in speed that my passengers had negotiated, I make some adjustments to our departure times. The changes will allow us the benefit of more time to explore the steep streets of Seattle and to find some good sushi.

My two companions giggle as they watch my pathetic attempts to use chopsticks. A sympathetic lesson comes quickly from Nakamura. He carefully guides the chopsticks into my fingers, "hold like pen and add second stick." It takes a few tries but I am pleased with my new-found skill as we consume a delicious variety of tasty raw fish. As we enjoy some sake, I tell them about our new flight times and both are pleased that we will have a little more time to explore at each stop. I ask about the status of their Russian entry visas. Nakamura's secretary has already received the required documents in Japan and has agreed to send them on to meet us in Dutch Harbor, Alaska. According to my new plan, we should arrive at Dutch in two days from now, which should work out perfectly. As we walk alongside Pikes Place Market, the home of the first Starbucks store, we look out over the Puget Sound and watch the sun set. It will be the last full sunset we will see for several days as tomorrow we will head north towards the Arctic Circle and begin to chase the midnight sun.

It is smooth at our cruising altitude after an early start the next morning. The coffee is beginning to kick in and my mind starts to drift as the two turboprop engines hypnotize me with their synchronized drone. I stare down at the stunning snow covered mountains and glaciers below us in contented silence. The sheer weight of snow compresses the glacier ice and causes a bright aqua blue color where it meets the sea. These strands of blue ribbons are easy to see, even from my vantage point 20,000 feet above. I trace each of the huge rivers of glacial ice as they weave around the mountain peaks and up into the snow pack range. It is a stunning sight to see as we fly north along the coastline towards Anchorage, Alaska. We are chasing the sun. The tilt of the earth in these latitudes creates a bizarre phenomenon that plays havoc with your mind. Almost 24 hours of constant daylight during the summer and perpetual darkness in winter months. It is summertime right now and so we are guaranteed a complete lack of visual clues to trigger our bedtime tonight.

The arrival and landing into Anchorage is a relatively easy task and we are soon being driven in a stretched limousine, courtesy of Nakamura. After checking into our hotel, we decide to explore the beautiful mountains around Alyeska and then do a little local shopping in the old railway town of Anchorage. When we get back to the hotel, it is late evening but the sun is still shining as the three of us head out for food. As we sit overlooking the Cook Inlet, named for Captain James Cook after his 1778 expedition of the area, we raise three glasses of beer and clink them together as the clock strikes midnight. Sure enough, the sun is still shining low on the horizon. My brain is yelling for rest and so we are soon back at the hotel for our welcomed "sunny sleep."

Next morning, I complete the paperwork required to clear customs and we set off across the Bering Sea for the island of Amaknak, some 700 miles to the west. Many of the islands along the Aleutian chain are covered in cloud although the ocean remains relatively clear. Amaknak Island and the port of Dutch Harbor is no different, with low cloud and gusty winds present as I begin the challenging approach to the small runway. I am pleased when we break out of the cloud base exactly where we should be, over the inlet and between the mountains with the runway just off to my left.

Even Yamashita applauds my effort but the elation will not last for long.

It is a little chilly on the ramp under the overcast sky after I park our King Air next to a rusty hangar. My smile disappears as an airport worker gives me some news that changes everything. Apparently, there is no jet fuel available as the fuel delivery vessel has been delayed. "When will it arrive," I ask. "About a week, or two," he says. My heart sinks when I remember our upcoming appointment with the BAMOK intersection. It might take me another ten days to get a new entry permit from the Russians and so I begin to troubleshoot. The nearest available Jet-A is at Cold Bay Airport, some 200 miles back along the Aleutian chain towards Anchorage. But I don't have enough fuel on board to safely make it to Cold Bay and still have a safe reserve. The only other fuel is 450 miles to the west, so that is out too. I resign myself to the reality; we are stuck. "Maybe you should have called before you left Anchorage," the ramp worker adds. I'm annoyed at the obvious comment, but he is right and it is a lesson learned.

I must figure a way out of this embarrassing predicament otherwise we could be stuck here for weeks. I calculate that I need around 90 gallons of fuel to safely make the flight to Cold Bay plus have enough to return to Dutch Harbor should the weather go down during the approach. Somebody at the airport has an idea. An electricity company keeps a helicopter in a nearby hangar and he believes that they keep a reserve tank of jet-fuel somewhere on the airport. I call the helicopter pilot. He is more than willing to help me out but he only keeps 15 gallons in the tank for emergencies. I am running out of ideas. As I walk back towards the terminal I see something out of the corner of my eye. A large white truck is driving along the perimeter road; it's a heating oil truck. That's it! Jet-fuel is basically paraffin heating oil with some anti-icing formulas added. I run back into the terminal to find the airport worker. He tells me the name of the heating oil company and I call them. There is no answer but the worker knows where the truck driver is heading and so I catch a ride to the fishing harbor to meet him.

On the dockside, next to a dozen large crab boats and fishermen repairing stacks of crab pots, I shake hands with the truck driver and the deal is done. I have just bought 100 gallons of paraffin for the same price as the jet-fuel would have cost me. This is our ticket out of Dutch Harbor and I arrange to meet the driver at the airport in the morning. Back at the hotel, I share the good news with Nakamura and Yamashita, who are happy as we enjoy a great buffet of the freshest fish I have ever tasted - straight from the fishing pots to the table. Unfortunately, the package containing my two passengers' Russian visas has not arrived but after a few telephone calls, it appears that the package was incorrectly delivered to... of all places, Cold Bay! Nakamura tells the package company to keep it there for collection tomorrow. I finally begin to relax and head out to explore this beautiful, remote island.

The smell of fish is, at first, overwhelming but you quickly get used to it. In fact, according to a local guidebook, the port of Dutch Harbor is America's busiest fishing port in terms of fish landed on the dock. The natural harbor first attracted civilization here over 9,000 years ago, when the seagoing Unangan people first inhabited the island to take advantage of the protected inlet that remains mostly ice-free during the winter. In modern times, the first to settle here were the Russians, who defeated the Unangan people and put them to work hunting fur seals and sea otters for export. One of the oldest Orthodox churches was built in Dutch Harbor in the mid 1800's. It is still an impressive sight on the rocky shoreline with its large striking green cupolas pointing skywards.

Most people are aware of the Japanese bombing of Pearl Harbor during World War Two but few are aware that there was a second harbor bombed. The Japanese successfully bombed and occupied Dutch Harbor just six months after the Hawaii bombing, until the end of the war brought fishermen back to fish for Bering Sea King Crab, Pollock and whitefish. The volcanic skyline of the island is simply breathtaking, when you can see it. The weather is very unpredictable and can deliver extremes in a matter of hours. When skies are blue and visibility is clear, the large number of colorful bird species flying overhead turn most visitors into amateur ornithologists. The most striking and impressive bird on the island is the Bald Eagle, of which there are ample to be seen around the harbor. You can normally hear them even if you cannot see them, although it is easy to mistake their call for a kid playing a Kazoo!

The next morning, I finish hand pumping the 100 gallons of fuel into the wings of our King Air, taxi out and line up on the short runway as the thick fog begins to roll in. My arms are still aching but I am keen to get airborne. There will be no coming back to Dutch Harbor as I can only see a few of the runway lights in front of me. If I am unable to land at Cold Bay, I'll have no choice but to keep flying on towards Anchorage and land at King Salmon Airport instead. I run the engines up to full takeoff power while holding the brakes to ensure that our new fuel is satisfactory. The acceleration is strong and we are quickly in the air, climbing above the fog into blue skies. With a slight tailwind, our flight is swift, albeit in the wrong direction. After landing, I set about refueling with almost 350 gallons of precious jet fuel in Cold Bay as my two passengers retrieve their Russian visas from the terminal building. I look at my watch but I really can't believe what I see. If we leave Cold Bay within the next twenty-five minutes we will have time to fly to Adak Island, refuel and fly onto BAMOK intersection on the early side of our original entry time. Finally, things seem to be going right.

I quickly load up and get back into the air, this time pointing towards Russia. Flying west along the Aleutian chain is an impressive journey. Almost every island has a prominent volcano or the remains of a volcano rising high into the sky. The Bering Sea sits to the north of the chain and the Pacific Ocean to the south. On this flight along 550 nautical miles of the islands, I count eleven volcanic peaks over 5,000 feet. The last of these peaks, a 5,710ft peak on Great Sitkin Island, is one I hope to avoid as it is inconveniently placed right on the approach path to our destination at the former Naval Air Station on Adak Island. This is our last available airport before we land in Russia, with "available" being the keyword. There is a runway on Shemya Island, between Adak and Russia, but Shemya is the home of a powerful COBRA DANE intelligence gathering radar owned by the US Government. Ferry pilots and any other "nosey parkers" are not welcome!

The straight line flying distance between Adak Island and our Russian fuel stop at Petropavlovsk Airport is just under 900nm. Our King Air has a safe range of around 1,150nm. However, the Russians have insisted that we follow part of their antiquated airway route, flying from one ground based navigation beacon to another instead of flying directly to the destination using GPS courses. This bureaucracy adds another 100nm to the route and so I am pushing our King Air close to its endurance limit. I make sure the fuel overflows our wing tanks before we leave Adak, and taxi fast to the runway. As we level off at 22,000 feet, I check the navigation computer. It shows us arriving overhead BAMOK at 2:04pm, eleven minutes early. More importantly, it shows us landing with a little over fifty minutes of fuel remaining. The leather seat in this elegant aircraft has never felt so good as I sit back, amazed at how our string of bizarre occurrences have led us to being in the right place at the right time. As we close in on BAMOK, the American controller passes us to the Russian controller.

The ocean still looks the same, the sky is still the same color, the wispy high clouds are still visible but things have most certainly changed. We have just entered Russian airspace. First, I adjust my altitude a little so that I can report our altitude in meters. Second, the clear radio transmission of the last controller is replaced by a scratchy, broken broadcast as the Russian controller barks a few orders at me, sounding as if he is talking into a tin can. It doesn't matter to me, we have crossed the BAMOK intersection on time and my passengers light two more celebratory cigarettes behind me. I smile and turn twenty degrees to the left toward our next reporting point. It is less than ten minutes later that I notice a concerning number on the navigation display. Something doesn't make sense to me. How can we be landing with only six minutes of fuel remaining? Where is our fuel going? Do we have a leak?

My heart rate increases as I check my progress logs and realize what is happening. A stronger than expected headwind is pushing us back and so we are using much more of our precious fuel to fly towards Petropavlovsk. I beg the controller for a more direct course but he insists that I stay on the assigned route. With or without his permission, I know I must cut the corner to avoid becoming a smoking hole in the ground. The "on and off" transponder trick will help to divert his attention a little as I shave a couple of miles from the various turns I have been assigned to fly. But then, the left engine LOW FUEL light illuminates and the right engine light quickly follows. Yamashita sits next to me having seen the light from his seat in the cabin.

Without saying a word, he assesses and understands what I am doing and approves with a nod. I turn the transponder off again to try and gain another couple of miles in our favor. "I'll delay our descent and go down with idle power to the runway," I say to Yamashita. He nods his approval of my plan. "You must return to course," it's an order from a different Russian voice. "Correcting, so sorry," I say. I turn a couple of degrees towards the approved course before switching the transponder back on. I let Nakamura know the situation and inform him that I will declare an emergency if we receive any delays on the approach. If I can possibly avoid broadcasting this word, I will avoid a lot of paperwork, questions and additional delays. However, if our safety is in doubt, I won't hesitate. We are all in agreement.

As the largest active volcano in the Northern Hemisphere passes off our left side, I briefly marvel at the sight of such a perfect inverted "V" shaped mountain, topped with snow and rising over

15,500 feet above the Kamchatka Peninsula. Gray ash is still escaping from the very top of the volcano and it is abeam the volcano that I have planned to begin my descent. I pull the throttles to idle and begin a steep descent, converting some of our altitude into a few extra miles towards the airport without using extra fuel. The volcanoes decorating the landscape ahead lead to a long green valley and the crystal-clear Kamchatka River. I try not to become distracted by the stunning view outside as I turn to line up with the light gray runway, still with the engines at idle. "We must be running on fumes." I let out a huge sigh of relief as I settle the wheels onto the concrete and taxi to shut down next to the old Russian terminal building.

A welcoming face greets us as I open the aircraft door. It is my friend Valery who will help us deal with the various bureaucratic agencies and speed up our transit in exchange for a "few gifts." Most corporate aircraft have a mini-bar and almost all the corporate aircraft I have delivered are well stocked with small bottles of various liquors. But, the contents will rarely make it to their destination, especially if a stop in Petropavlovsk is scheduled! I check with Nakamura and a nod authorizes the exchange. Valery's full shopping bag "clinks" as we walk into the old terminal building and up a flight of stairs to his office. The process is swift, there are handshakes all around and we are soon airborne again heading for Japan.

My two new friends smile as I ease their beautiful aircraft onto Japanese soil for the first time. The airport of New Chitose, in the north of Japan, is huge and I taxi for several minutes to reach the customs area. Greeting us is a group of people dressed in white chemical suits. One comes straight to the cockpit and points a plastic yellow gun at my head! Seeing my obvious distress, Yamashita explains that they are simply checking for a fever; the "gun" is a thermometer. Next, the customs people ask for a sample of fuel from our tanks. I fill a half-gallon jar and watch as they carefully weigh the liquid to ensure they oan correctly charge the right amount of tax based on the exact weight of the fuel we are carrying in our wings. Last, a Shinto priest performs a ceremony to purify the trusty King Air to ensure that good spirits will watch over her. I shake my head when I receive the bill. The handling cost for this stop is over $2,000 and I can't help but wish that the Japanese would accept payment in miniature liquor bottles too.

After two more short stops, we land at our destination of Kohnan, in the south of Japan. I am sad to bid farewell to my two Japanese friends. Despite my initial concerns, we have had fun and experienced quite an adventure together. I didn't realize then that an incredible surprise is waiting for me at home. I open the envelope to find two return tickets for my fiancée and I to join Mr. Nakamura and Mr. Yamashita for a personal guided tour of Japan. Of course, the first stop on our "tour" is appropriate. We stand together where the first atom bomb hit, at the International World Peace Site in Hiroshima. Our heads are bowed as we pay our respects.

The King Air on the ramp at Dutch Harbor Airport, Alaska

SIXTEEN BARS

Cirrus Design SR22
USA, Canada, Portugal, Senegal, Gabon, Namibia, South Africa
(8,250nm 65.5 flying hours)

"It's the worst place for this to happen. I tell Graham that I will fly next to him and let the rescuers know where to look after he crashes. A malfunction is rendering his ferry tank unusable and he doesn't have enough fuel left in the wings to reach our destination, five hours ahead in Namibia. Sixty miles to our left is the coast of Angola, which is in the grips of a civil war. Graham and his passenger have a simple choice; ditch into the shark infested South Atlantic or land in a war-zone. I wonder if I am watching the demise of yet another ferry pilot friend."

It is two months after the Yak delivery: My friend Andrew has asked me to test fly a beautiful "V" tail Bonanza he wants to buy. It belongs to Graham, a cheerful South African living in central England. Graham shows me around his Bonanza and we are quickly flying north to meet Andrew at an airfield close to his home in Scotland. Graham and I hit it off immediately as he is also a ferry pilot and we are soon telling tales and comparing notes on some of the people we have met while ferrying; the good, the bad and the ugly! Graham tells me about a quandary he is facing with his next ferry job. He has been asked to fly two Cirrus SR22s from the United States to South Africa. However, the dealer needs both delivered together and Graham doesn't know another ferry pilot with Cirrus experience. "Well, you do now," I say.

The following week, we meet at the Cirrus factory in Minnesota to begin our journey to South Africa. I have flown many single engine aircraft across the North Atlantic to Europe but this will be my first time to Africa. My mind conjures up images based almost entirely on the Tarzan movies I saw as a kid. One thing is for sure, Africa will be much warmer than Minnesota, it is absolutely freezing here. Our first task is to fit the long-range fuel tanks into the back of the two aircraft. We meet Joe at the Cirrus factory. Joe is an experienced ferry pilot and a very respected ferry tank installer. He is a Minnesotan native whose smile seems to get bigger as the temperatures drop. I complain a lot about the cold but this just seems to get Joe more excited. He demonstrates his party trick by filling a cup with boiling hot water and throwing it into the night sky. It is so cold outside that the hot liquid falls as snow! I have never seen anything quite like this and I'm both amazed by the trick and baffled as to why anyone would want to live here!

It is my first time in northern Minnesota during the middle of winter and the outside air temperature is a ridiculous -36°c. I always complained about the "bloody cold" of England but this is cold on an entirely different scale. My breath seems to freeze as it leaves my mouth and the wind scorches my exposed skin as we walk across the slippery ramp towards the two new aircraft. I agree to help Joe with the tank installation and so we fly in loose formation to Sky Harbor Airport, ten minutes from Duluth. The tiny airport sits on a peninsula of Lake Superior and it is only just wide enough to accommodate the runway and a few hangars. Joe's girlfriend,

Candice, is waiting for us there. She is a California girl but has been in Minnesota for some time now. She too has this strange desire to be out in the cold. I am delighted when we finally close the hangar doors and warm up next to a heater.

Installing a large aluminum 110-gallon fuel tank is a job done with precision and great care. First, we remove the rear seats and build a wooden support platform to hold the tank in place. Then we fit the plumbing to allow the ferry tank fuel to flow to the engine through a small valve secured between the two front seats. Finally, we install the tank and secure it with some extremely heavy strapping. The job takes a few hours to complete and we are quite tired after finishing the installation for both SR22's. An FAA inspector will arrive in the morning to issue flight permits for the modified aircraft and so I am ready to go to my hotel and sleep. Joe offers to drive me.

These are the early days of my business and money is tight. Turning a profit is challenging and so I am thrifty when it comes to expensive items such as hotels. I always pick the cheapest room in town. A pillow and shower is all I really need. Joe pulls into the motel parking area and I quickly think I may have made a mistake. The motel reminds me of the opening scene in a horror movie. A large and squeaky rusty sign sits atop a slanted wooden pole, which has obviously been hit by a vehicle at some time. There are still bits of the crashed car at the base of the pole. Many of the room windows have been boarded up, as have parts of the roof. We look towards the office, guarded by a fierce looking dog. The tobacco stained yellow curtains reflect part of a blue neon sign, "NCY" - the only three letters of the word "vacancy" that still work. Nobody utters a word and Joe drives off. "You are staying with me, my friend," he says and we set out toward an isolated forest northeast of Duluth.

The last few hundred yards of his family land are the bumpiest. Joe's rusty car, nicknamed "Ole Shitty" creaks and groans as we negotiate the last few boulders before finally reaching our stunning destination. It is late at night and we are far from any light pollution, which makes the night sky above remarkably bright. The tree line of the Cloquet Forest is clearly visible where the stars begin. If I look straight up, I can fill my eyes with nothing but bright stars. I see a star moving, it's a satellite passing directly overhead. I could stand and stare all night but the extreme cold forces me into the small log cabin where Joe has already started to build a fire in a small iron furnace.

This cabin was built by Joe's family several years ago using only trees that have fallen in the surrounding forest. The firewood comes from the same source. As Joe, Candice and I sit around the cracking and popping fire, some soothing guitar music plays from a wind-up radio sitting on the window ledge. In no time at all, the cabin is warm and comfortable and we drink, talk and laugh until we cannot stay awake any longer. I fall asleep to the sounds of the forest and a lifelong friendship is firmly established.

When I wake the next morning, Joe and Candice have already been out for a walk. They are smiling and happy, meaning it must still be bitterly cold outside! After breakfast, we drive back to Sky Harbor to meet with Graham and his passenger, Piet. Piet has recently opened a Cirrus dealership just outside of Johannesburg and these two aircraft will be the first to arrive at his showroom. For Piet, the chance to fly along on the delivery flight is an opportunity too good to miss. I don't have my normal survival suit with me and there is much giggling as we struggle into the bright orange survival suits we have rented for this trip. None of them fit properly - I am too skinny, Graham is too tall and Piet is too short! We are soon packed and ready to leave for the first ten-hour leg to St. Johns, Newfoundland. Candice gives me a small piece of driftwood from Lake Superior as a good luck memento. I add it to my bag of growing lucky keepsakes that I will never ferry fly without:

> *Lake Superior Driftwood*
> *WW2 Memorial Coin from England*
> *Rock from Nuuk, Greenland*
> *Gander Aviation Coin*
> *Volcanic Rock from Iceland*
> *Japanese 50 Yen Coin*
> *Metal Fragment from Goose Bay*
> *Polished Stone from Alaska*

As the sun sets over Canada, our loose formation of two aircraft is making good progress. Graham calls me on our communication frequency. He is starting to pick up some ice and wants to climb. I also have some traces of ice and willingly follow him to 13,000ft where the temperatures should be too cold for the ice to stick to our wings. A few minutes later, the ice is continuing to accumulate and so we decide to divert to a nearby airport. The snow is falling hard as we break through the final cloud layer and see the runway lights of Gaspe Airport on the Gulf of St. Lawrence. A cup of hot coffee in the weather briefing room gives us the chance to warm up and see where this unexpected snowstorm is heading. If we fly twenty miles north we will be clear of it. Armed with this information, we refuel and load up again. Within two hours, we are back in the air and three hours later we are enjoying a beer at a local St. Johns bar.

The next morning Graham and I are seated around a large table at the airport, planning the next leg. Half way between St. Johns and the African continent is a small group of volcanic islands, the Azores. Refueling on one of these tiny Portuguese islands is the only option available to us as there is nothing but ocean for rest of the 1,200nm flight. If we are unable to land because of weather or any other issue, we will not have enough fuel to make it back to St. Johns. A decision to continue or turn back will be made in-flight, at the PNR – the point of no return. We calculate this point using a formula that considers fuel endurance, speed and the forecast winds. We mark the PNR as a thick black line on our chart at 5 hours and 49 minutes into the flight. For clarity, I draw the "skull and crossbones" flag next to the PNR line on my chart. It is essential that we receive a good weather report for landing before we reach the PNR.

The latest Azores forecast says that there is a chance of a little scattered mist at our estimated arrival time and so we will need to check the weather several more times before we reach the PNR. Graham and I pack up the charts and head out to our planes with Piet. As I settle into my seat, I look around to ensure my essential items are with me: large empty apple juice container, bottles of water, peanuts, lucky charm bag and cans of soup. Not being a fan of cold soup, I always push a couple of cans onto the floor close to the cabin heating outlets. After five or six hours near the heater, the soup is lukewarm but good enough to enjoy! There is some self-induced psychology involved with my soup heating practice. Long oceanic flights often become very tiring and boring. If I encounter bad weather during a crossing it can mentally drain me. Knowing that my soup is warming gives me something to look forward to and reminds me that once I pass the halfway point every minute flown is another minute closer to landing. I always look forward to opening my can of lukewarm soup during my ferry flights.

Santa Maria is the most easterly island in the Azores and it is our destination today. I get airborne and settle into my ferrying routine. I keep a meticulous note of my fuel burn and check it by using an old ferry pilot method. I place the back of my hand at the top of the ferry tank and then slowly move my hand down until I feel the cold of the fuel inside. I draw a mark on the tank at this point for comparison to my calculations. This gross error fuel check is surprisingly accurate. We are approaching five hours of flying time and all the engine parameters are fine as we close in on the PNR. Graham uses his satellite phone to check the weather in Santa Maria. I look down and see a huge cargo ship being tossed around by the huge Atlantic swells. The sea is particularly nasty today and I plot my position on the chart next to the pirate flag I drew earlier. I am anxious to hear the weather report from Graham. The weather is acceptable and so I cross the PNR and open my can of lukewarm soup to celebrate. We are now committed to land at Santa Maria.

Unknown to us, the temperature is dropping rapidly in Santa Maria and the mist is thickening, but it will be several more hours before we find out. I scramble for the instrument approach chart when I finally hear the marginal weather conditions relayed from the airport tower. With no radar available, the approach must be flown without assistance from air traffic control. Flying an instrument approach this way demands following a certain set of published instructions exactly to ensure separation from terrain and a successful feed onto the extended centerline of the runway. It goes something like this:

Start at a known point and fly an exact track, compensating for wind before descending to a specific altitude. At a certain distance, make a turn and descend a little more. Start a stopwatch. At a designated time, turn again and capture a radio beam, which will lead to the runway. Descend into the foggy darkness and stop at a few hundred feet above the ground to look for the approach lights.

The concentration required to fly this procedural approach is very high, especially after a tiring ten-hour flight. Errors made when flying these types of instrument approaches can be deadly. In 1989, a Boeing 707 crashed at Santa Maria while flying this very same approach. Confusion with the charted altitudes killed all 144 people on board and I hope I will not make the same mistake. The approach goes well and as I level off at 600 feet above the ground I can see the runway lights ahead of me. Graham has already landed and gives a thumbs-up as I taxi in next to him. The local Azores beer is famous for being brewed in the back of a church. We celebrate our successful leg by enjoying a few pints of *Especial*.

The sky is blue and welcoming the next day. We have a little time to explore Santa Maria. Settlers first came to this ten by six-mile island in the 1200s. The island was so prone to attack by pirates that almost all visitors were initially treated with hostility. In fact, when Christopher Columbus landed on the white sandy beach on his way back from discovering the "New World", the locals captured many of his crew and imprisoned them! Our welcome has been far more agreeable and we are sad to leave the cobbled town streets and light brown clay chimneys that dot the landscape. However, I am itching with anticipation to leave for Africa. Graham and I calculate the PNR for the next leg and we set off for our flight across the eastern Atlantic, planning to fly just to the south of the Canary Islands and on towards Africa.

My first glimpse of Africa is a little bit of a disappointment. There are no jungles, giraffes or lions on the horizon. Instead, I see the dusty city of Dakar on the Atlantic coast. The city sprawls out into a "burned brown" color desert surrounding the metropolis of low buildings and concrete. There is ample heat and humidity at 9,000 feet as I make my approach to the airport. The rising thermals make my little Cirrus bounce around but I soon touch down on the African continent for the first time. I am excited to get out and explore but as I shutdown the engine two African men walk towards me with machine guns at their sides. Again, not quite what I was expecting but I soon discover that they are security guards offering to keep an eye on our planes in exchange for a few dollar bills. A few more dollar bills go to the customs agent and the immigration process is similar - dollar bills and smiles. It appears that this part of Africa is run by the constant exchange of dollar bills.

When we walk outside the airport terminal, pandemonium erupts. Hundreds of locals jostle to get to the three of us. We are white men with money and the mission of the crowd is to encourage us to part with some of our cash in exchange for any service they can offer: translator, taxicab locator, bead seller or spiritual advisor! Graham, Piet and I are pulled from one person to another, quickly losing each other in the bustle. As I open the door of one taxi, another man pulls me away and shoves me into a different car. We race off with a dust trail following closely behind us. I wonder whether I am in a cab or being kidnapped? The man sitting opposite me is smiling. He has self-appointed himself my guide to Dakar and introduces himself as Mbaye. He seems pleasant enough and I guess his age to be 20. As we weave through the sand-filled streets, I see that we are driving through a large shantytown. The thousands of miss-match shelters are constructed with various bits and pieces of junk. Children and ragged dogs sit outside some of these jumbled homes. Most buildings have a rusty corrugated iron roof and I have no idea how many people live in each of the structures as I begin to feel a little self-conscious. I now understand why there were so many people waiting for us at the airport. The people here are extremely poor and they are simply looking for any work or way of earning some money. I'm sure that the crummy hotel in Duluth would seem luxurious to them. I catch sight of a few faces through the car window. Nobody seems too bothered by their surroundings or by the car that is flying by with me staring out. We slow a little and I wave at a few of the kids standing around; they wave back. I wonder what a typical day might bring for these kids. I want to meet some of the locals but Mbaye cautions me against it.

We turn onto the road leading to our hotel. Large golden gates are opened and in the space of 200 yards, we drive away from desperate destitution and into obscene luxury. The gates quickly close behind us, shielding the guests from the "real-world" outside. I literally shiver with guilt and embarrassment. I absolutely hate this. Soon, Graham and Piet turn up in another taxi, complete with their own version of Mbaye. I want to get out and see the real Dakar and so does Graham. Mbaye arranges transportation while we shower and change clothes.

It is good to be clean and I'm ready to set out and explore. I explain to Mbaye that we want to see the authentic Dakar, where the local people go for a beer and have a good time. Unfortunately, he focuses in on one phrase, "good time." We bump along endless potholed dark streets heading deep into town and I begin to wonder if I have made an error. Perhaps we should have stayed at the fancy hotel bar with Piet? We finally arrive at a small building with various people standing outside smoking cigarettes. A few neon lights from the windows light the dark street outside. It seems like the type of place a Dakar local might come to relax but the reality hits us when we walk through the door.

The narrow smoky room has a long wooden bar stretched along the right side of the wall, with several rows of liquor bottles hanging on the wall behind. Standing next to the bar are a dozen scantily clothed black ladies. I look around the room and see a few old couches pushed against another wall. There are two men being shown a "good time" by some mostly naked girls. Horror fills me, especially when I realize that Graham and I are the only two white people in the bar. I know that we should not be here but it's too late as the girls have seen us. The volume drops as the huntresses lock onto their prey. I walk towards the bar, acting as normal as possible and trying not to lock eyes with anyone. Immediately, two or three girls leave their clients and push up against us. I order a beer, as does Graham. I feel dirty, claustrophobic, and use my outstretched arms to mark my space at the bar. Disease is at the front of my mind and I want no part of this. Four or five black girls are standing around me as I sip my beer and I attempt to usher them towards their clients who are waiting on the couches. One persistent young black girl thrusts herself against me and lowers her top in a desperate move to encourage a purchase. I look over at Graham, who is getting a similar treatment. We nod an acknowledgment and quickly head for the door.

Two larger men are less than pleased with our thrifty visit and they begin shouting in a language we do not understand. "This can't be good," Graham mutters. We stand our ground and allow the men to release their anger just a few inches from our faces. We do not flinch. Mbaye is nowhere to be seen. Desperate to escape, we flag down a passing cab but within minutes the driver drops us at another dismal bar full of prostitutes and pimps. He is obviously receiving a commission like the first driver and Mbaye were. We demand that we be taken back to the hotel. Our attempt to see the real people of Dakar has failed. Graham and I are the last to leave the hotel bar but I have developed a new attitude; I have had enough of people pushing us around here. The next morning, I order a taxi driver to take us to the airport, "no middle man required." I barely look out of the window as we drive by the same dusty streets. I wish we had simply walked out of the hotel and spent our evening with the people who live outside of those grand golden gates but I am glad to be leaving Dakar.

Most countries require prior permission to transit their airspace and Africa is notoriously slow at issuing these "overflight" permits. We have yet to receive a permit to fly into airspace controlled by the Ivory Coast. "Never mind, we will route around them," Graham says. This next leg from Senegal to Gabon will now involve a substantial dogleg to avoid flying over the Ivory Coast. It is going to be a very long flight but we have little choice if we want to keep making progress towards South Africa. We leave in the evening to avoid some of the largest thunderstorms, which reach their most ferocious during the daytime. So much for my great view of Africa! We fly from dark navigation beacon to dark navigation beacon until we are overhead Accra on the southern tip of Ghana. The large town below glistens in the night as it is the only illuminated area in this part of Africa. There is nothing else to look at as we drone on into the darkness towards our destination, Libreville. The Gulf of Guinea is 9,000ft below us and in the distance I can see some intensifying flashes of lightning.

Our two aircraft are only a couple of hours from the coast of Gabon and my large ferry tank is now empty of fuel. I switch a valve that directs the main wing tanks to supply fuel for our final push. The flashes of lightning ahead are becoming brighter and far more frequent. The long route around the Ivory Coast has left us very little fuel remaining to be able to dodge the storms ahead. In the lead plane, Graham suggests a plan. We will push though the storm at right angles, accept some turbulence and hope for the best! It isn't a particularly brilliant plan but I know it is the best one we have. I tighten my seat belts and head for the middle of the storm, hoping that it is a narrow band.

Navigating through thunderstorm lines is quite familiar to me and it is usually a predictable exercise. This storm is no different. First, the radio fills with a loud static sound and then the turbulence increases violently as we enter the outskirts of the system. Flashes from strikes further away light up the clouds all around us and I turn up the cockpit lighting to protect against flashes momentarily blinding me. As we get closer to the core of a storm I can smell the electricity well before any lightning will strike. This is a ferocious system that disrupts my vision with every jolt, making the instruments quite useless. I close my eyes for several seconds at a time, trying to realign my internal balance. With each lightning flash, I look for a hole in the cloud, or at least a horizon to confirm whether I am still flying the right way up. After a few minutes in the storm, I settle into a basic routine and I know that if I have survived this long I'll probably get out ok. Without warning, a deafening crack passes through the little Cirrus. This one is substantially bigger than the other strikes and I wonder if I have been hit. I look around to see if there is any visible damage. I can smell a little burning but most of the instruments appear to be powered and the lights stay on. I wonder about the structure and whether it has been damaged. The little Cirrus is flying ok for now and I hope it will last until I can reach the end of this brutal storm. After a few more minutes of heavy turbulence and blinding flashes, Graham says he is in the clear. I exit the system right behind him, fatigued but still flying. I can see the lights of Libreville in the distance ahead. Relief fills me as Graham calls the tower for our clearance to land. Our eleven-hour flight will soon be done.

"Denied," is the response from Libreville control tower. Graham tries again. "You do not have permission to land," they say. We both know that the controller is playing a game, one that he hopes will end with a payment, but we have a legitimate permit to land and so we choose to ignore him. There is simply nowhere else for either of us to land and so with or without permission we decide to land anyway. As expected, a jeep full of shouting people are there to meet us, with machine guns at the ready. We know the game and we have already armed ourselves with ammunition; rolls and rolls of one-dollar bills. Eventually, we pay each of the men off, ten dollars at a time. It's a silly game but we are rapidly becoming experts.

In a loose French accent, the immigration officer demands to take possession of our passports during our stay. After much argument, I throw my passport onto the table not expecting to see it again. This results in an immediate pointing of guns. Piet summons his best French, "S'il vous plaît accepter mes excuses?" They begrudgingly accept the apology and the guns are lowered. I don't often lose my temper but I have simply grown tired of playing this ridiculous game. Without our passports, we walk to an unfinished airport hotel for what will be a short sleep and no food. We bribe the hotel Manager for rooms with locking doors, which locks the mosquitoes in with us too. I am covered in bites within minutes. My African dream isn't going so well.

The next morning, we are ready to leave without delay. We arrive at the immigration office and the uniformed officers play dumb when we ask for our passports. We expected this and the rolls of one-dollar bills are once again used. As they finally hand me my passport, I see a sight that horrifies me. Several women and children are lying on the floor of the immigration office. Some have obviously been beaten but I don't know by whom. I demand an explanation from the officer. He does not answer but waves me away with his gun. This time I don't really care and I order them to release these people. The officers begin to laugh and mutter to each other. I stare into the eyes of one officer and quickly realize that he holds no value for their lives or for mine. He cocks his gun without any change in his facial expression and he waits for my response. With no other option available, I back down and plead that he treat these people with respect. I feel sick to walk away from the fifteen or so women and children in that room but another officer eases my mind a little by explaining that they are in Gabon seeking asylum from a neighboring region and that they would be "fine." I didn't know whether to believe him and I know that the image of these people lying on the floor surrounded by an intimidating armed militia will never leave me.

I really hate this place. I wish that I had followed the advice of a ferry pilot friend. "Outrank them," he told me. This seemed silly at the time but now I understand what he meant. "They only respect rank down there." He said that whenever he travels through these parts, he doubles up the normal 4 shoulder stripes of an aircraft captain. "With sixteen bars on your shoulders, you'll outrank everyone and they won't know what to do!" I wish I'd listened. I bribe the fuel man to "find" the key for the fuel truck and he fills our two-aircraft ready for the longest leg of our journey, south to Namibia. As we get to the runway, the tower controller cancels our takeoff clearance. He tells us that we need to speak to the Head of Security before we can depart. Graham has already bribed enough "Heads of Security" and so we ignore the instruction and simultaneously apply full power.

My engine sounds rough as I gain speed along the runway. It has developed a random "popping" noise, but it is still producing power and I am less than enthusiastic to stop. There it is again, another pop. Perhaps it's a misfire? I pull my headset away and listen closer. The noise is coming from behind me. Oh, my God, are they are shooting at us? I look back and see one person shooting a rifle into the air. I cannot believe that they are doing this but I'm sure it is a scare tactic and I refuse to fall for it. I am relieved to lift into the air at 6:30am local time, just as the sun is rising. "Bang!" The noise scares the shit out of me. Have I been hit? I look around but it's just the passenger door that has popped open. The suction of the airflow outside prevents me from closing it. I check the aircraft manual to see if there is a closing technique when airborne. The book instructs me to "land as soon as possible." As soon as possible will be another eleven hours flying time ahead in Namibia, and so I fly on.

To avoid flying over the war-torn country of Angola, we fly twenty miles from the coastline and over the southern Atlantic Ocean. I establish a loose formation with Graham and we soon cross the Equator. My celebratory "equator soup" is perfectly lukewarm. After a few more hours, Graham radios me to tell me he has a problem with his ferry tank. This really is a terrible place to have this kind of problem as there are so few options available. With so little fuel left in the wing tanks, we both know he will never make it to friendly Namibia. Graham elects to fly close to the beach and wait for his fuel to run out before gliding to the ground. So many thoughts are running through my head. Should I land too and provide safety in numbers? If Graham and Piet survive the crash landing, will I ever see them again? Who can I call to help recover them? I realize that I don't even know if Graham has a wife or family and I decide that it's not a great time to ask. I stay close to their stricken Cirrus, waiting and watching for something to happen. An agonizing fifteen minutes

149

goes by before I hear "it's flowing again, let's get out of here." Thankfully, the problem has rectified itself and Graham suspects a temporary blockage from dirt in the bad fuel we received in Gabon.

We cross the border into Namibia and fly over land once more. Our approach into Windhoek is stunning. A landscape of darker sand, a few patches of green and a horizon spotted with small dark brown mountains greet us. The long black runway is a welcome sight and I walk across to shake Graham's hand as soon as my engine stops. He has used a life and I know he is lucky to be alive. Namibia is different to the other African countries we have visited. As a former German colony, it is well organized, clean and shows little sign of corruption. The hotel is spotless, the people are friendly and there are no threatening machine guns being pointed at us. This is more like it!

We have traveled almost the length of Africa but I finally feel that I am seeing the place I first imagined. Before the sun has a chance to set, I walk to a higher vantage point and look out into a vast valley. The beautiful golden sands of the Kalahari Desert flow far into the distance, weaving around the bottoms of tall, dark and ragged mountains. The evening sky is clear and the temperature is warm. There is far less humidity than there was in Dakar and Libreville. Looking down at the airport, I can see our two Cirrus's parked next to a beautifully restored Douglas DC6, with polished aluminum panels that catch the colors of the setting sun. I sit for almost an hour, staring into the distance and listening to the unusual sounds of the desert preparing for nightfall. I wish I had time to explore tomorrow but we will be leaving early for our destination in South Africa.

The friendly immigration people wave us off the next morning and we set course towards Johannesburg. The Kalahari looks different at sunrise, more golden and less dusty. Half way to South Africa, we cross the Zambezi River and fly across our last African country of Botswana. It is here that my original vision of Africa are realized. As I peer down from the cockpit of the Cirrus, a large herd of wildebeest is charging across the sands, leaving a long dust trail behind them. I try to see if anything is chasing behind them but the stream of sand blocks my view. The majestic sight of this vast land and the animals that inhabit the area surrounds my small cockpit windows and I recline my seat back a little to take it all in. I feel incredibly privileged to witness such immense natural beauty from my vantage point above. This is the Africa I dreamed about and the one that I hoped I would see for myself. It is magnificent and I would be happy to fly around here all day.

After a journey of over 8,000 miles, we finally land at Lanseria Airport just to the north of Johannesburg. A small crowd is waiting to greet the first two Cirrus SR22s to arrive in South Africa. Piet is happy and he drops me at his house while he and Graham organize our airline tickets home. Piet's home is in the style of a Mediterranean house except there are huge iron gates at the entrance. I turn on the TV to discover what South African's like to watch. I am disappointed to see *The Jerry Springer Show* playing and I decide to go out for a walk instead. I lose myself and soon find a barbershop. It seems like a good time to get a trim and so I enter. The four black ladies stare at me and do not say a word. I assume they don't speak English and so I gesture scissors with my fingers, smile and sit in an open chair. Not a word is uttered as one of the ladies grabs a straightedge blade and cuts my hair. She motions for my approval after finishing and smiles as I give her an "ok" sign. I leave some money on the side with a good tip.

Piet falls back into his chair in shock when I tell him where I found the barbershop. "You can't go there, you're white," he says. "I'm surprised they didn't murder you!" Apartheid has recently ended in South Africa but many are slow to adjust from decades old rituals. Piet guesses that the silence in the shop was probably a genuine reaction of astonishment as their first ever white customer walked in. I chuckle to myself. It was probably the best haircut I have ever got.

Just before leaving the Azores for Africa

ICELAND DRIPS

British Aerospace ATP
USA, Canada, Iceland, England
(4,655nm 22.7 flying hours)

"Fuel is gushing onto the ramp like a waterfall. I shout and wave my arms to encourage the fuel man to hit the emergency stop button. I run across the icy ramp for some sand to begin soaking up the mess. The Icelandic authorities have already seen us and a small car with a yellow flashing light on top is speeding over to our airliner. A short man in a bright orange safety vest jumps out of the car and begins yelling. I ignore him and continue heading for the sandbox. He blocks my way and declares that we are grounded. He demands that I surrender my pilot license. I need a plan."

It is one year after the King Air delivery: I have just received a quote request from a guy who seems to know me but I don't know him. In the email, I'm thanked for the great job I did "last time" but I have never heard of this guy. I read on anyway. "Please deliver three British Aerospace ATP airliners from the desert in Arizona to England," the sender asks. The largest aircraft I have ferried thus far had twelve seats and a fifty-foot wingspan; the ATP is a sixty-four-seat airliner with a 100ft wingspan. It's probably out of my league - or is it? I sit back in my chair and ponder the idea. The export paperwork, planning, permits and routes will be just like any other aircraft I have ferried. I turn to the world map hanging on the wall behind me and locate the departure city and destination. Next, I cut a piece of string equal to the approximate fuel range of the ATP and begin to work out a rough route. It seems familiar enough. I am convincing myself that the size of the aircraft doesn't seem to matter and so I respond to the e-mail with my quote. A signed contract arrives before the end of the week and I begin planning.

Almost immediately, a problem arises. These three aircraft have not flown in over four years and they are the last of this model left in the United States. No pilots in America are current on the ATP and no simulator exists in America to help regain currency. How on earth am I going to fly them out of the desert? Luckily, I have a good relationship with several people at the FAA and so I ask the question. An FAA inspector understands my predicament and offers me a lifeline. As a private flight without paying passengers, the regulations are not as stringent as those for the airlines. "Find one of the pilots who last flew the plane, and if they are current in an aircraft of similar size do 3 takeoffs and landings before you leave and that will satisfy me." This is great news. All I need to do is track down a pilot who flew one of these airliners to Arizona four years ago.

I set off to find the aircraft logbooks with my ferry pilot friend Joe. To ease the workload of this unusual delivery, I employ Joe to help plan the flights and, of course, share the fun. After checking the logbooks, Joe gives me two pilots names. They are both in managerial positions at US regional airlines. The first has too many work commitments but the second is interested and I make an offer. "I'll pay you up front, in cash, and you'll be back to work on Monday morning." John is in. Joe and I plan the details of the flight and I obtain permits and insurance. Things are starting to fall into place. Next, I must ensure that the three aircraft are airworthy, legal and safe to make the long journey back to England, so I leave for the Arizona "boneyard."

As a small business owner, I wear a staggering number of hats. I am the accountant, marketing manager, secretary, website host, flight planner, permit agent, handling agent, meteorologist, HR department, tea boy, client communications, filing clerk, customs export agent, and pilot. I'm meticulous with my paperwork. Delays that arise from having incorrect paperwork can make or break a delivery. I even print the export papers on the exact shade of "government" yellow paper so the customs agents are comfortable with something that looks familiar. I have found that if the paperwork pack looks right, most assume that it has been completed right. This allows a much quicker process and obtaining an approving "red stamp" from the customs officer is a satisfying validation of my thorough preparation.

The mechanics employed to prepare the first ATP for the ferry flight have been working for almost five days when I arrive in the hot and dusty Arizona desert. We are due to depart tomorrow and a new FAA inspector is overseeing the airworthiness authorization process. I ask the mechanics for an update on our authorization but I cringe when I see how badly the paperwork has been prepared for the inspector. I will require a "pink slip" ferry flight permit to enable us to fly the old airliner to England. It's quite simple - no pink slip, no flight. The inspector is the only person who can issue this "pink" FAA form. As with most bureaucrats, any attempt to hurry will guarantee a snail's pace service but the mechanics have been calling his office constantly and threats have even been issued! I am horrified when I hear this. In my experience, this is the worst way to deal with the FAA, so I drive to the inspector's office to offer my apologies and assistance. I expect a frosty reception when I walk into his office but I see a Monty Python poster on his wall and I pounce. I start a conversation about the English comedy gang and discover that one of his favorite sketches happens to be one of my favorites too! We laugh and shake hands. I have little doubt that our precious "pink slip" will arrive before we are due to leave tomorrow. Next, I meet John at the hotel. He looks exactly like the TV character Niles Crane from the show Frasier. John is keen to fly and has only one request for me, to buy a case of Diet Pepsi for the trip! John is literally addicted to the stuff and the thought of flying multiple hour legs without his precious drink is, to him, unthinkable. A quick trip to the local Walmart solves that issue and a celebratory beer is consumed before we sleep.

Tumbleweed rolls across the dusty ramp as I walk towards the ATP next morning. I feel like I'm in a scene from a western movie, with the jagged red rocks surrounding the dusty isolated airport. I am also a little apprehensive as I am responsible for ensuring that this large machine and those on-board make it safely to England. I stand under the fuselage and look up. This will be the longest day of flying the old aircraft has ever undertaken. I wish her luck, give her a pat and begin the ferry flight. The plan is to fly to England with three short fuel stops in Minnesota, Canada and Iceland. There will be three pilots on board; John, Joe and myself. We will each take turns to fly in a planned rotation throughout the night to keep everyone fresh and to help keep things on schedule.

We will be under the command of John for the entire flight and I will be responsible for both the paperwork and managing the ferry flight.

Joe and I have already received our familiarization training on the ATP systems and so I begin to set-up the cockpit and arrange the aircraft manuals in a logical order behind the co-pilot seat. As I reach around to retrieve a performance manual, my hand brushes against something and then it feels like my whole arm has entered a raging fire. It's like nothing I have ever felt before. A small spider has thrust its fangs into my skin and is now scurrying for cover. Within minutes, my hand begins to swell quite badly. A lady at the airport terminal thinks it might be a black widow or brown recluse bite and she wraps my hand in a hot compress. For the next couple of hours, she watches me like a hawk and continually engages me in conversation. Luckily, it appears that the spider didn't have the opportunity to give me a significant dose of its venom and my hand slowly begins to return to its normal shape by the time the FAA inspector turns up with our "pink slip."

John is completing his final cockpit checks as I load the bags with the equipment and supplies we will need during our flight. Survival equipment, "check," aircraft documents, "check," selection of tools, "check," crew luggage, "check," Diet Pepsi, "check." I close the cabin door as John completes the start sequence before he carefully moves the two tall thrust levers forward, generating a deafeningly high pitch whine from the engines. With no paying passengers on board, the large airliner rapidly speeds down the runway with dust billowing behind us and is airborne before we are half way down the runway. Finally, we are on our way.

I spend the first leg of most delivery flights learning the personality of the aircraft. During the take off and climb, my eyes are rapidly scanning the instruments to check that things are running as they should be. I check where each needle on each gauge sits to ensure any changes are easily identified later. Are the engine instruments matched? Is the pressurization working? Has the autopilot captured correctly? What is the rate of climb? Are the fuel flows correct? Once at cruise altitude, I sketch out the position of the instruments to set benchmarks. If anything looks different during the delivery, I will check back on these drawings and carry out a quick comparison. As we climb today, I also look over at John. With his thousands of hours of experience flying this aircraft, it is good to see him comfortable and content. The spectacular Grand Canyon is passing below us and I gaze down at the morning mist pouring around some large red rock structures that tower over the vast landscape of Arizona. I peer deep into the huge gorges cutting through the desert, fascinated by the different colors painted by Mother Nature over the past few million years. There is no cockpit chatter as we all absorb the stunning view through our privileged windows.

"Get me a Diet Pepsi, will you Steve," John says as we get settled into the cruise. I go back to the small cargo area behind the cockpit but the door is locked and I can't find the handle. I am puzzled. I remember loading the bags, manuals and Diet Pepsi using this door, so why can't I open it? Oh no! I recall something I read about this door. The ATP is designed to allow ground handlers to load last minute bags using this cabin door but a one-way lock prevents passengers from accessing the cargo area while in flight. I sheepishly return to the cockpit empty-handed. "Right, we will land then," John says! I accept that this was my error but the cost of fuel and time will be huge for the sake of a brown fizzy drink. I put my foot down but also ask what might happen if he doesn't get his liquid hit. "I get irritable, angry, violent and unpredictable!" I am fifty one percent sure that he is joking.

Thankfully, during the next few hours, John stays calm and we soon begin setting up for our approach. I now learn why some pilots nickname the ATP "Another Technical Problem." Approaching Duluth, John asks for the flaps to be lowered so that our approach speed will be slow enough for landing. I reach down and move the large flap lever but nothing happens. Apparently, this is an irritatingly common issue with the ATP and so John says, "there is a manual deploy handle in the box of tools, get it and lower the flaps using that." Embarrassed, I remind John that the toolbox is also locked in the forward cargo hold with his Diet Pepsi. There's no other option but to land without flaps extended and so John increases the landing speed to account for it. With light snow drifting across the Minnesotan runway, the ATP smoothly touches down and our first leg is complete. As the two large propellers wind down, the demand from John is expected, "Get me my Diet Pepsi!"

Within an hour, we have cleared customs, refueled, filed a flight plan and are flying towards our next stop. The sun is starting to set and we nestle in for a five-hour flight to Goose Bay. Halfway between Duluth and Goose Bay is a small collection of lights in the middle of nowhere. It is a remote town with a fabulous name, Chibougamau. The name means "Gathering Place" to the native Indian Cree people who have lived in the area since the 17th

Century. Cruising at 300mph, the lights of Chibougamau pass by quickly and it isn't too long before we are within radio range of Nickki at Goose Bay. I relay our estimated time of arrival and ask Nickki to order three large cheese pizzas for our hungry pilots. The plane and pilots are quickly refueled and we continue towards our last fuel stop in Keflavik, Iceland.

This delivery is going very well and I am pleased with myself. I have successfully applied the lessons I learned while delivering smaller aircraft to this larger aircraft delivery. The mood on board is happy and we are comfortably ahead of schedule. I decide that I like delivering these bigger aircraft. The payout is higher, the safety level is increased and flying with several other pilots is fun! When I finish this delivery, I will push to get some more of these "easy" airliner jobs. Of course, a slap of reality is waiting for us in Iceland.

We are forty minutes from beginning the approach into Iceland. I am talking over the plan with John and Joe. If we can land, refuel and be back in the air within one hour, we will have a chance to fly to England and make a commercial flight back to America a whole day early. The enthusiasm for this plan is high. Everyone is assigned a task for the upcoming fuel stop. I will deal with the customs paperwork, John will deal with the flight plan and Joe will deal with the pre-flight inspection and cockpit set-up. John lands on the huge runway with snow banks piled each side, we pull into the FBO at Keflavik and shutdown the engines. The clock has started.

My good friend Ty is waiting to help us. He is quickly clued into the plan but I make a mistake. "Fill her up," I enthusiastically shout to the fuel man as I rush pass him on the way to the customs office. I have forgotten that we only need to fill ¾ full at each stop. John and I had talked about this back in Arizona. After sitting in a dry desert for many years, some of the rubber seals in the old airliner were cracked and most were replaced. But one set of seals was deemed unnecessary for our delivery, the fuel tank seals at the very tips of the wings. The wings on the ATP angle upwards from the fuselage, which keeps the fuel at the bottom of the tanks. In Arizona, I calculated that we would never need to take a full fuel load for any of our legs. We only need a three-quarter fill at each stop. Never filling the tanks means the fuel never reaches the end of the wings and so there was no need to replace the very outer wing seals. The FAA inspector had agreed and was happy with this. However, in Iceland my miscommunication to the Icelandic fuel man leads to a cascade of fuel flowing out from the ends of both wings. "Stop, stop," I shout as a large volume of fuel gushes out. An angry airport official is now out of his little car and is still yelling, announcing to us all that the aircraft is unsafe to fly and we will have to answer to the Icelandic authorities. I manage to avoid handing over our pilot licenses but I cannot change the fact that we are grounded. We finish spreading sand to help soak up the spilled fuel and secure the ATP for the night. The fuel is still leaking when we leave but at a much slower rate than before. I book some rooms at a local hotel and call the Director of Aviation Safety to personally apologize. He allows me to explain and he seems much more reasonable than the angry airport official. He asks me to come to their offices in the morning. I agree as I really have no other choice.

At the hotel, John and I get together to discuss a plan. We will have only one shot at getting our presentation right and so we put on our thinking caps. I overheard a couple of interesting pieces of information at the airport and I share them with John. First, the "angry" airport official was the person who filed the report on our incident. I do not have a copy but I understand that he has wildly exaggerated many of the details. He has described a "massive leak" lasting for almost an hour. This is untrue as I know that the bulk of the flow lasted for no more than a few minutes. I was confused about why this person would want to fabricate his report, and that led to the second piece of information. Apparently, the official has only worked at the airport for two weeks and he has already annoyed several people with his attempts to make a name for himself. I am prepared to take full responsibility for the spill and I feel bad for the trouble it has caused but I also know that our leak was not on the scale of the Exxon Valdez spill! I want to ensure we keep the incident in perspective and we stick to facts. John and I assume that the Safety Director must know of the "ladder climbing" ambitions of the airport official and so we decide to play on this a little.

Our plan is to be completely honest but also a "tad" sneaky. We decide to continually downplay the report sent by the official at every opportunity we get. We intend to do this by fully supporting his "obvious enthusiasm" but also highlight his "obvious inexperience." We will suggest that his perception of the volume of fuel may have been clouded by his unfamiliarity of the ATP itself. I then plan to introduce John as one of the most experienced ATP pilots in the world and ask the Director to listen to his expert view, hoping that this will trump the contents of the questionable report. John plans to explain that an occasional fuel "weep" is very common for this type and does not pose a flight safety issue; this is a factual statement. I

164

also plan to encourage the Director to come and see the "massive leak" for himself. Of course, we will only expect to see a very few drips by tomorrow morning, which we will point out to the Director. I will also offer to cover the entire cost of the clean-up, with my apologies and I hope that this plan will allow us to leave without any more delays.

We finish dinner and I head back to my room to prepare a document pack for the Safety Director. Bureaucrats seem to love a lot of "blame deflecting" paperwork to justify their decisions and so I prepare the pack in the same meticulous way I produce my customs paperwork. I take a great deal of care to present the documents in an organized and logical order, fastening everything together in a professional looking binder. Luckily, the hotel front desk helps with my stationery items. I am pleased with the pack, which contains copies of certificates, licenses, permits, authorizations and insurances with relevant sections already highlighted. I believe that I have included everything the Director will need to make an informed and comfortable decision, and hopefully allow us to continue with our journey.

It is early the next morning. John and I are having coffee with the IAA Safety Director. We have already completed our pleasantries and so I begin by offering my sincere apologies for the event and extend my offer to cover the full the cost of the cleanup. Knowing that the tone will not be confrontational, the Director seems to relax a little. He listens as we maintain the coolest heads possible to explain the issue while ensuring that we show support for his airport staff and the "excellent" safety work they do. As the Director thumbs through the document pack, John explains some of the common operational issues with the BAe ATP, including the known fuel weeps. After a short time, we all shake hands and our offer to the Director to come and inspect the fuel leak is accepted. At the airport, we all stand under the wing and I am keen to point out a couple of drips falling from the lower seals. I suggest that this dripping does not really constitute a "massive leak" but, praise the enthusiasm of the official who reported the leak.

"Ok, you must pay 7,000 Króna to cover the cost of clean-up," the Director says. I do a quick calculation in my head and realize that this is less than $100. I thank him and apologize for taking up so much of his valuable time. I walk up the aircraft stairs and close the main door. As soon as we are airborne, the relief explodes in the cockpit. High-fives, cheers and fist bumps fill the small space. John and I are extremely happy that our professional approach has ended with a timely departure and a very small fine. I feel guilty for staining the Icelandic ramp but I know that the outcome could have been much worse if we had not had a solid strategy and taken time to prepare.

The last leg to England is the most satisfying. As we touch down, the sense of achievement flows. ATP number one is home and two more are waiting back in Arizona to be collected. I keep the same team and two weeks later we meet back at the same hotel in the same desert, ready to collect the ATP number two. I construct a flight plan that has us landing in Iceland around 2am local time. I am hoping that the angry official in his little car with the flashing light will be safely tucked up in bed when we arrive!

The two-remaining aircraft are delivered with slightly more familiar and traditional issues for Atlantic crossings. We have some small hydraulic fluid issues, propeller governor problems and a few oil leaks. Within a few weeks, all three ATPs are back in England, on-time and on budget. The customer is very happy and he chuckles when I confess that his original quote request was sent to the wrong person! I return to my small desk and I am filled with pride at having successfully delivered my first three airliners. I also know that my reputation has been strengthened as several more quote requests have arrived for larger aircraft. The unexpected identity error and an old leaky ATP have allowed me the opportunity to turn a corner with my ferrying company and I am so glad that I never deleted that email.

One of the British Aerospace ATPs during a delivery

BROKEN WING

Piper PA28 Archer
USA, Canada, Greenland, Iceland, England
(4,590nm 43.7 flying hours)

"I can't believe what I see as I peer inside the small cabin and look at the floor just behind the two front seats. The mechanic has removed the floor panels and points to the metal wing spar. There is a crack running down the beam that holds the wings of this plane together. I wonder how much this crack had grown during the pounding turbulence of a particularly aggressive Atlantic Ocean. I am angered by the deadly fracture and I have questions. Who caused this, who knew about it and why did they send me off across the ocean on such a suicidal ferry flight?"

It is one month after the ATP delivery: I am in Florida to pick up a very nice Piper Archer for delivery to England. The larger aircraft deliveries are fun, more profitable and safer but most of my ferry flying still involves flying small private aircraft like this Archer. It is wintertime but the sun is so bright that it is almost impossible to see without sunglasses. The small four-seat aircraft looks immaculate on the ramp, dressed in an elegant red and white paint scheme. It is well equipped too: color GPS with a moving map and a full stack of bad weather instruments including a "storm-scope." Not many aircraft of this size have one of these clever little devices that can detect and display electrical discharges from thunderstorms. I'm

169

sure that the "storm-scope" will come in handy for my Atlantic crossing. I review the airframe and engine logbooks, confirm that the export airworthiness release has been signed and I set off on my next delivery flight.

My first stop is in Alabama, where my fiancée, Andrea, is working as a veterinarian at a local zoo. We are planning to attend a wedding in New York later this week and that just happens to be along my delivery route, so I decide to fly us both in the Archer. We drive out to the little Alabama airport, ready for our flight north. It is a little stormy when we arrive, which is quite typical for this time of year. The light brown leather seats will be comfortable for the eight-hundred-mile flight. I turn the key to start the engine – but nothing happens! I try again, but the battery is completely dead. If I can get the engine running, the alternator will recharge the battery while we fly. I give Andrea a quick lesson on the cockpit engine controls and I go outside to take the place of the electric starter motor. An aircraft engine can be started without a battery but it requires that the propeller be swung by hand. It can be a dangerous task without training but I have "hand-propped" many aircraft in the past and so yank the propeller through several times until it finally catches and the engine starts. A few hours later after our first stop, the same thing happens. The battery obviously needs to be replaced and so I order one to be available for our arrival into New York. For the next few stops, I swing the propeller to start the engine. Andrea has fun flying the little Archer for much of the flight to New York and we arrive at the wedding with plenty of time to spare.

It is back to the business of ferrying the next day. The battery has already been replaced and Andrea has left on a commercial flight home. I fly on my own across New York and onto Maine to have the ferry tank installed. The standard Piper Archer has enough fuel to safely fly for around four hours. I will need at least eight hours of fuel to safely make the short hops across the Atlantic using my normal "good weather" route of Canada, Greenland, Iceland and England. However, if the weather turns bad I will need to take the long route direct from Canada to Ireland, which will require closer to sixteen hours of fuel. The Atlantic weather is very unpredictable at this time of the year and so I decide to have a 115-gallon fuel tank installed for this crossing. As normal, the rear seats are removed and the tank is installed in their place. The tank control valves are placed next to the pilot's seat.

The extra weight of the fuel puts the little Archer slightly over the normal maximum authorized weight and so an FAA inspector arrives to sign some additional paperwork to make the delivery flight legal. It is already late afternoon in Bangor, but I want to get on my way. I squeeze my luggage and survival equipment around the large ferry tank and set off towards Canada. Night falls quickly as I fly north. The weather forecast shows some areas of freezing rain along my route and so I am not surprised when I run into some icing conditions three hours into my flight. The little Archer does not have de-icing equipment and so I am unable to continue flying tonight. I use the GPS display to find the closest airport among the surrounding mountains and head towards it.

Below me is an airport I have never heard of before, *Du Rocher Perce Airport*. The approach to the Quebec airport is rough and turbulent but the short runway comes into view at 1,200 feet above the ground. After I shut down, it appears that I am the only person here and the town seems to be some distance away. I cover myself with my jacket to protect against the cold pouring rain and I run over to a small wooden hut. I need to find a hotel for the evening and luckily there is a payphone inside but I quickly realize that I have made a rookie mistake. I have not brought any Canadian quarters for use in the phone, The hut seems warm enough and so I run back to the plane, retrieve some of my survival equipment and return to make a bed for the night. I fall asleep quickly.

Sometime later, the lights in the hut are turned back on, startling me awake. There is a man and a lady standing over me and I hear a car idling just outside. They smile and seem friendly. The lady explains that they heard me fly overhead and so decided to stop by to ensure that I landed ok. They offer to drive me into town and I gratefully accept. It is still dark and it is raining quite hard as we drive the few miles along a coastal road to the small town of Chandler. I know I have crossed the border into Canada as the road signs passing outside the car are written in French. I thank them both for dropping me at the small hotel and I am soon back to sleep in a warm hotel room.

I awake in a sweat and check the time. I have been asleep for over twelve hours. I feel sick and I am sure that I have a fever. I decide not to fly today and I call down to the front desk to extend my stay. I spend the next two days in bed listening to the rain outside and watching French language soap operas on the small television in the corner of the room. After three days, I still don't feel great but I simply can't stand to sit around any longer. I am also conscious that the aircraft owner is patiently waiting for his Piper to turn up and I don't want to delay any more. I take a long shower to cool off and take a taxi back to the airport. The rain has stopped but it is extremely gusty at the small airfield. I file my flight plan and depart for the familiar stop at Goose Bay. Again, it is turbulent on the approach and each bump makes my bones ache. My internal autopilot takes over the flying as I am struggling to concentrate. Luckily, I know this route like the back of my hand but I know that I can't possibly head across the Atlantic tonight. I still feel awful; my nose is blocked and my head feels like it is going to explode. After I land, Nickki calls Linda at the B&B and I head off for some more rest. I sleep for another thirteen hours but awake the next morning feeling much better. Linda's wonderful greasy breakfast goes down well and a large coffee puts me back into the right mood to fly so I spread the Atlantic plotting charts out on her kitchen table to begin planning my crossing. The weather is not particularly great across the ocean today and there are several weather fronts crossing my path. I know that I will be earning my money on this delivery.

Having an accurate weather picture is essential before I head out towards the ocean. Winds are always first thing I look at. I will go out of my way to find a tailwind and avoid a headwind, even if that means flying into bad weather. Any headwind means burning more fuel, which gives me less opportunity to fly around thunderstorms. The tailwind is the strongest at 11,000 feet today and so I choose this as my crossing altitude. The winds are not strong enough to allow a direct crossing and so I plan a fuel stop in Greenland. Given the time of year, I am guaranteed some areas of uncomfortable flying conditions and the weather charts confirm this for my first leg. Beyond Greenland, there are some storm systems forecast on the way to Iceland but they should not prevent me from flying. I expect that the conditions will change during my flight and so I will be meticulously monitoring the conditions as I fly. As always, I will log the actual air temperature, wind strength, wind direction, my fuel state and engine parameters every fifteen minutes. This information will help me decide on any route and altitude changes I need to make as I fly east towards Europe.

It is 2am on a very cold and wet morning at Goose Bay Airport. I am wrapped in several warm layers of winter clothing and I have just finished my pre-flight checks. I am leaving early to try and capture as much daylight in the storm area as possible. This will give me the best chance of picking my way through the worst thunderstorms and maybe see where the highest build-ups are. Having the little "storm-scope" will be a comfort on this crossing and it will help me to see where the most active storms are located. The overnight temperature dropped well below freezing, which has turned the engine oil into a substance as thick as treacle. A heater has been warming the engine compartment for about an hour. It's basically a very large hairdryer, pumping hot air into the engine compartment through two long yellow tubes connected to the air intakes at the front of the plane. I head for the flight planning room for a last-minute check of the weather radar, satellite picture and synoptic pressure charts. The winds for the first half of my flight demand a stop in Narsarsuaq, on the southern tip of Greenland. I draw a route line onto my map and file the oceanic flight plan, listing each waypoint and an estimated crossing time for every 5° line of longitude. I will cross three longitude lines, 60°W, 55°W and 50°W during this 776-mile leg.

I am ready to leave and so pull on my bright yellow rubber survival suit and place a can of soup near the cockpit heat outlet. My rubber suit is smelly and uncomfortable but it could keep me alive for a few vital minutes if I have to ditch close to a potential rescuer. I pay careful attention to the zipper on the front of the suit. A ferry pilot recently crashed into the sea off of St. Johns and he survived the impact. Helicopters were on their way to collect him but he had not zipped his suit properly and the freezing cold Atlantic water poured in. He lost consciousness and drowned before help could arrive. The ramp guys remove the heating tubes and I quickly start the little Archer. The howling wind is blowing straight down the runway, which makes it easy to coax the heavy flying bomb into the cold morning air. There is no autopilot and so I will be hand flying for the next several hours. I make a turn towards my first reporting point and adjust the fuel mixture to ensure a warm engine with a lower fuel consumption. I watch the engine instruments carefully as I climb. Student pilots are taught to check that their engine instrument needles are "in the green" band. For these oceanic flights, I need early identification of any potential engine problems and so note exact numbers instead.

I am slowly climbing to my cruising altitude and I begin to compare the outside environment with the forecast weather maps to see how accurate the charts might be today. My can of soup is warming nicely and I open a bag of roasted nuts. I always drink a lot of water during my ferry flights, which means that my large empty apple juice container must be close by. As I climb, the changing pressure makes the ferry tank pop and bang behind me, a familiar sound to mark the start of an Atlantic crossing. I level off at 11,000 feet and plot the first few position fixes onto my map. I check the engine instruments again and listen closely to the engine, quietly searching for any irregularities. I am soon out of radio range and my last VHF position report has been filed. It is still dark but the sun will rise ahead of me in a couple of hours.

As the day breaks over the Atlantic, I experience an incredible feeling of loneliness and isolation. I am surrounded by ocean as far as I can see. I feel very insignificant as I look down and stare at the splashes of white spray on the top of the ocean. From this altitude, they look so small and innocent but I catch sight of a large container ship being tossed around by the angry swell. It's comforting to know that other humans are close by and I subconsciously turn a few degrees towards them. It is a clear day with very little cloud cover. Every now and then, an airliner contrail disturbs the featureless view above. I feel tired but my body does not allow me to sleep. Occasionally, my head finds itself resting against the side window but the vibration quickly shakes me back to my job. Boredom sets in very quickly and keeping my fifteen-minute flight log up to-date helps to keep my brain active.

A few hours later, the white caps of the ocean are dotted with solid white icebergs as I approach the western Greenland coast. There are three distinct valleys carved deep in the mountains ahead. Every Atlantic ferry pilot knows these valleys. I aim for the middle one, which twists and turns its way to the airport at Narsarsuaq. The other two valleys dead-end with no room to turnaround at the ends. I fly low into the valley between huge snow-covered mountains rising each side of me and watch some large icebergs pass below me. It is a magnificent sight and I could fly around here all-day long. As I round one of the turns, a large rock sits just to the left of the valley. It's several hundred feet high and it fills me with sadness every time I see it. This is the rock that killed Simon. He was flying a Piper Archer like this one when he ran into bad weather in the valley. It's a healthy reminder that danger is all around despite being so close to the destination. Soon, the valley opens into a much larger fjord with smaller icebergs scattered around. I can see the single runway at Narsarsuaq Airport sitting at the far end of the fjord and beyond the airport is a large aqua-blue glacier that rises thousands of feet straight up into the permanent Greenland ice cap. It is one of the most incredible approaches in the world and I love flying into Narsarsuaq.

After I shut down the engine, I walk to the top of the control tower, past the seal-fur boots sitting in the shoe rack. The storms towards Iceland have become impassable and so I call it a day and head for the nearby *Hotel Narsarsuaq*. I chat to the barman, who remembers me from another trip. I tell him of the fever I had in Canada and the irritating cough I have been left with. He makes me a local remedy, a "Greenland Coffee." He grabs a clear coffee glass and describes the drink as he makes it:

"First, pour Kahlua to represent the earth's crust. Then top it with Tullamore Dew whiskey to denote the fjords and pour on the coffee for the land. Plenty of whipped cream on top represents the icebergs and finally, some flaming Grand Marnier to symbolize the Northern Lights above."

It is early the next morning on the tip of Greenland. The good weather has left and the sky above me is gray and angry. The swirling clouds are evidence of the whipping winds that exist aloft. I will be working hard today and enjoy a large breakfast before I fly. I head back to the control tower to begin my planning. There is a whole bunch of mixed up weather between here and Iceland but the favorable winds will help to reduce my flight time and give me plenty of fuel to deviate from my course if necessary. The departure from Narsarsuaq for these types of small aircraft is very challenging and it is vital that I fly accurately when cloud cover exists between the mountains like today.

I takeoff toward the fjord and start a constant spiral climb above the airport using exactly twenty degrees of bank. I enter the cloud and keep the spiral going upwards. I must stay exactly over the airport as I climb and I use a radio beacon to check my position. I can't see the mountains for the clouds but I know that they are right next to me. I check to see if any ice is forming on the wings. There is none as it's too cold for any precipitation to stick, meaning ice crystals simply bounce off the wing. There is a lot of turbulence trying to throw me off my spiral but I trust my instruments totally as the constant turning has rendered my own sense of balance inoperative. I reach an altitude of 9,000 feet and turn to a heading of 070 degrees, almost due east. This takes me out of the valley cloud and towards the ice cap.

The correct name for the ice cap is the "Greenland Ice Sheet." It covers most of Greenland and is over 1,500 miles long and over one mile thick in places. At 9,000 feet, I feel as if I can reach out and touch the top of it. The last few hundred feet of jagged mountaintops poke through the cap, leaving me to wonder what the rest of the buried mountain must look like below. Perhaps people will see these mountains many centuries from now as the earth warms and the ice melts? There is no sign of life across the cap, just miles and miles of pack snow between random pieces of rock. Flying so close to the top of the cap gives a great sensation of speed. With the tailwind pushing me along, the little Archer is flying at almost 170mph. Despite this, it still takes over an hour for me to fly across the cap and find myself over the Atlantic Ocean again.

I can see the telltale signs of bad weather ahead of me. A line of black cloud stretches from far left to far right and I check the "storm-scope" for lightning activity. It shows pockets of activity but there seems to be a few gaps that I can get through. The storms have formed here because several strong pressure systems have collided together and are feeding each other with a heavy mix of moisture and wind. The cloud base is lowering as I head for the first weather front so I pull my seat belt tight in anticipation of what is to come.

First, a heavy mix of rain and ice pellets smashes down on the windscreen like somebody sandblasting me with small rocks. Next comes the turbulence, violent and ferocious as it twists the little plane around like a toy. I can hear the fuel crashing around in the large fuel tank behind me. The heavy straps are holding the tank in place well. I look out of the window and see ice building on the wing. Decision: go up or go down? The benefit of flying over the ocean during a storm is the lack of terrain to hit. This gives me a much greater chunk of airspace to utilize before I will find the ocean. I decide to descend but it's a mistake. The ice collects rapidly on the wings and I briefly try to climb back up but the weight of ice prevents it. More ice begins to collect. I have no choice but to head down until I find myself just below the cloud base. The angry gray sea and white spray of the blowing wave tops are just 200 feet below me. I can barely see more than a few feet ahead. The windscreen is being battered by wind and rain. I am sandwiched between the ocean and the ice-maker above.

My airspeed is getting dangerously slow because of the weight of ice I am carrying on the wings and fuselage. Flying at this speed in these gusty conditions is causing me a lot of concern and I desperately need some more speed to have full control of the little aircraft in this turbulence. I can't believe what I am about to try but I am out of options. In a Newfoundland bar one night, an inebriated ferry pilot told of a technique he claimed he used to clear ice. I didn't believe his story at the time, but he swore to me that it worked. "You have to get *really* low and use the salt from the sea spray to soak the plane and remove the ice." I cannot think of anything else to do, and I must do something. I decide to give it a try and fly as low as I dare. The visibility ahead is appalling and the ocean below me is incredibly vicious. At about fifty feet above the waves, I lose my nerve and go back up. I consider my options again. I am flying dangerously slow and so I have little choice and nothing else to lose. I tighten my seat belt and try again. I concentrate as hard as I can, reacting to every move the waves make around me and trying to aim for a wash of spray. I scream out to myself "THIS - IS - INSANE!"

I am just a few feet above the wave tops now. I see it coming just before it hits me. A torrent of ocean spray soaks the little plane as I strain against my seat belt. I feel the immediate deceleration and wonder if I have hit the ocean top. The salt water drenches my windscreen and the wings. I cannot believe that I am still flying and the incredibly risky technique has worked! There is far less ice on the wings. The wind is blowing so hard that the spray from the tops of the waves soaked the whole fuselage. I hang in another spray area for as long as I dare. The ice is slowly melting away and I consider dropping another two or three feet to catch another big spray but I have lost my nerve. I head back up to the safety of the cloud base. My wings are clean and my airspeed is slowly recovering. I have no idea what to think and I am still in disbelief at what I just did. "That'll make a good story in a book one day, but nobody will believe it," I think to myself.

Slowly, and as expected, the cloud base begins to rise and I follow it up. The visibility improves dramatically and I complete another entry in my fifteen-minute flight log. The temperature has risen significantly and the winds have changed too. I know I am flying from a cold front to a warm front, as they stretch out from the strong pressure system to the north of me. I have made it through the cold front and I am heading towards the warm. I expect less risk of icing but much more turbulence. The little "storm-scope" has also become very active. The embedded storms don't look too bad ahead but they stretch out right across my path. It's going to be rough ride but I know that the worst of the weather will probably only last fifty miles or twenty minutes of flying time. I pull on my seat belt again and enter this next band of clouds.

Once again, the turbulence is horrendous. My legs ache from the constant pull of the lap belt. The control wheel snaps out of my hands before I can grab it again. The winds are frolicking with me, picking me up and then brutally throwing me back down. Every bone in my body aches and I am concerned for well-being of my poor carriage. The little Piper is being subjected to some of the worst turbulence I have ever experienced across the oceans. Twenty minutes seems to drag on for hours. Eventually, I exit the front and I find myself in clear skies again. I am exhausted and fatigued but turn my attention to the approach into Reykjavik. Before I begin my descent, I consider my engine It is running a little hot after working so hard in this freezing and inhospitable environment. I know that if I pull the throttle back now, the drastic temperature change will put extra stress on the engine components so I keep the engine RPM high and reduce the power very gradually during my descent to allow the engine to cool at a much slower rate.

Turning onto final approach, I catch sight of the huge spire on top of the Icelandic Church at Hallgrimskirkja. The striking white building stands almost 250 feet tall above the town and it is a welcome sight to see after this particularly challenging flight. My arrival into Iceland signifies the end of the onerous segment of this Atlantic crossing and a local "Viking" beer is an appropriate reward.

The rest of the delivery is uneventful and I am pleased to see the smile on the face of the new owner as I touch-down in England. David says that I can stay at his house for a couple of days while I wait for the tank to be removed. After that, he wants to do some conversion training in his new aircraft and learn how to use the various instruments. His house is incredible, a large country manor on a huge estate in the southwest of England. The tour of the manor takes almost half an hour. The main building was constructed near the end of the 1800s and contains some wonderful works of art. The house incorporates an original chapel, dating from the 1600s and the temperature change inside the chapel is very eerie so I am glad to get back to the warm house after visiting. The children are polite and smartly dressed. They are playing games when a bell rings and we head to the dining room for dinner. It is the first time I have been waited on by servant staff. I really don't know what to make of it. I'm uncomfortable but everyone appears to be happy and smiling, including the wait staff. I desperately want to talk to them to find out whether they really enjoy their job, but I never get the chance.

In the evening, the children arrange some entertainment for us. David and I help the three sisters put out a few exquisitely carved chairs for some family members who will be joining us. We receive our hand-written programs from the three girls:

Timetable: at 7:45pm, in the Library. Order: Hannah, Kate and Augusta will sing and dance "Barbie Girl", "Stop Right Now", "Baby Love" and "If You Wanna Be My Lover."

I can't help but compare their upbringing to my own. Just a few years earlier, I'd been living in a tiny mouse-infested room and showering in the sink. I wonder how they would react if I told them? I am brought tea in a china cup from the younger female servant and I sit back in a comfortable antique chair to watch the show. It is a lot of fun and the girls can't stop giggling as they receive thunderous applause from their appreciative audience. I sleep very well.

In the morning, David finishes a call to his stockbroker and we drive to the airport. The mechanic motions us over to look at something in the Archer. "It's bad news I'm afraid, a crack," he says. As I look at the cracked wing spar, I can't believe just how deep it is. The Piper is an incredibly strong aircraft and I am sure the turbulence across the Atlantic did not cause this. However, I do wonder how much the crack might have grown during the crossing. I ask if the installation of the ferry tank might have caused the damage. "No," the mechanic says. In fact, he believes that the even distribution of the weight of the tank over the thick spar might have helped to minimize the growth, The mechanic Is convinced that this crack existed before I collected the aircraft in Florida. Shining a flashlight up inside of the wing, he points out some aluminum patches and bent metal. Surely, I didn't miss such a large repair when I inspected the logbooks. "Well, that's the thing," he says, "there is no record of any damage in the logbook and there's certainly no record of this shoddy repair." The mechanics news is stunning. David is angry and he goes back to the house to call the aircraft salesman in Florida.

Several weeks later, David relays the story to me over the phone. It appears that somebody had taxied the Archer into a hangar door over a year ago. The wing suffered substantial damage but the repairs were made in secret, so as not to lower the value of the aircraft. It is probable that the crack in the wing spar was small enough to be missed during the patch-up but had grown during the next 75 flight hours. I am stunned. I realize that I have been incredibly lucky. One more storm may have pushed the crack to breaking point, almost certainly resulting in a complete loss of control. The thought that Andrea had flown in this unsafe aircraft also angers me. I salvage some satisfaction when I hear that one of the perpetrators has been prosecuted. He will never be allowed to touch an aircraft again.

Several months later, I return to fly with David in his newly repaired Archer. This little plane with its single propeller has already opened a window to so many different worlds: hot Florida, cold Canada, mountainous Greenland, ice pellets, ocean spray, arctic sun and monumental turbulence. And now, I am staring down at a green scrub topped hill leading to a long Scottish loch below. We are flying just a few hundred feet above some grazing goats as David sets up his approach to a remote airstrip and completes a perfect touchdown. He stops the engine and I open the door into the brilliant sunshine overhead. All is quiet, except for some bleating sheep. We are the only people for miles around. We lean against the sturdy wing in satisfied silence, absorbing the tranquility and fresh morning air.

Our social backgrounds couldn't be more contrasting but our mutual love of aviation has allowed us to share this wonderful moment. A shiny red and white Piper Archer with a broken wing has unexpectedly created a cherished friendship and brought great happiness to us both.

The Archer at a private grass strip in Scotland after repairs

BOEING JEANS

Boeing 737-200
USA, Canada, England, Turkey, Pakistan
(8,479nm 23.1 flying hours)

"We don't have enough fuel to make Karachi at this low altitude as the thick air is making our two old jet engines burn too much. If we can climb to a more efficient altitude, we might have a slim chance of making it but the controller keeps denying our request. Our only other option is to land and refuel in Iran. I wonder how the Iranians might react to our unannounced landing in a large blue airliner, sporting a prominent American flag on the side. I ask the stubborn controller for a higher altitude one more time but he tells me to standby. I turn to Les and ask how much longer we can possibly continue to standby. He looks as worried as I have ever seen him."

It is almost four years since my first delivery: Dials, levers and gauges fascinate me. When I was nine years old, I remember a class trip I took to a reconstructed Iron Age village in the south of England. The people at the village were dressed in period clothing and blacksmiths used primitive tools to make iron artifacts. There were goats and sheep all around the old mud huts and I helped to make a fire in one of them. When we returned to our classroom, we were asked to draw a picture showing the highlight of our trip. Much to the bemusement of my teacher, I drew the instrument panel of the bus that took us to the village! Twenty years later, the vast panel of buttons, dials and switches in front of me still gives the same thrill. I am sitting in a jet airliner from the generation before glass screens displayed the flight instruments. Every system has a button, a light and an analog display. However, this Boeing 737 cockpit panel has several holes where the instruments should be. In fact, almost half of the instruments are missing and we are supposed to be leaving for Pakistan tomorrow morning.

I stand on the rusty steps positioned against the main cabin door of the old Boeing and scan the California "boneyard" at Victorville Airport for our contact. Frederick claims that our aircraft will be ready for us to leave "first thing" in the morning but I think he is being over-optimistic despite his obvious confidence. It is hot and dusty in the desert today and I decide to go for a walk and look at some of the hundreds of old airliners parked around me. Row after row of abandoned aircraft are stored here with reflective material covering their windows to protect the interiors. Almost none have engines and many are missing wheels and odd panels that have been salvaged for other uses. Most of the silent fuselages sit on railway sleepers, which seems like quite an undignified end to me. I imagine how shiny and clean these jets would have been when they first entered service and how proud the pilots were to fly such modern aircraft. Now, decades later, these aircraft have been abandoned in the sun to await their fate. Many are sold for the value of scrap metal but others, like the Boeing we will fly tomorrow, are sold to less regulated countries where a well-used and noisy jet is still allowed to be flown.

My ferrying business is booming, I am employing other pilots and referring contracts to keep up with demand. I am pleased that I continue to receive quotes for wonderful airliners like the Boeing 737. Les was one of those who spent time convincing me to follow my dream and become a commercial pilot so many years ago. He was also the one who offered me my first airline job. Since then, he has retired from the industry and so I decide to turn the tables and offer him a job as my delivery pilot. Les and I walk out to the 737 early the next morning and find it completely ready to leave, instruments installed as promised. Frederick and I shake hands and I close the door as Les starts the two Pratt & Whitney engines. Ahead of us is 24 hours of flying time, including four fuel stops before we reach our destination in Pakistan. We plan to stop in Duluth (USA), St Johns (Canada), Bournemouth (England) and Ankara (Turkey) before landing in the second largest city in the world, Karachi.

As we climb out of Victorville, the Grand Canyon is clearly visible below us. It is such a stunning view and it seems a shame to have one hundred empty passenger seats behind us. We level off at 35,000 feet and I begin to relax a little. Les turns to me and says "stewardess, I'd like a coffee please." "Why yes Captain, right away," comes my response. I have ferried so many different types of aircraft over the past few years that I believe I can figure out most systems. However, no matter which order I press the faded colored buttons on the coffee maker, I just can't seem to make it work. *ON* is a given but where is the "brew" button? All I see is *WARM*, *WATER*, *LOW* and *LMP*. I refuse to be beaten by a coffee maker and so I make a guess. Warm first, and then turn on the water and push *LMP*, just to see what happens. Nothing happens and I eventually give up returning to the cockpit empty handed. Having no coffee for a seasoned airline pilot like Les is not a great way to start our trip and his look says it all. I promise to buy him a large coffee in four hours, when we get to Duluth.

It is a typical winter evening in the northern city of Duluth. The fast-moving drifting snow is blowing at right angles across the runway. It creates a bizarre visual illusion, making me believe we are traveling sideways when the bright landing lights illuminate the tarmac. After we shut down the engines, I open the cabin door and the freezing cold air enters the cabin. "After you get my coffee, you can do the post-flight exterior check, and make it thorough," comes the instruction from a grinning Les. This is obviously my punishment for being outsmarted by that stupid coffee maker. I come back into the warm cockpit with icicles hanging from my nose. Les still has a smile on his face and I know he is hiding something from me. He giggles as he tells me he "just remembered" that the coffee maker water was disconnected in California! Saying nothing, I go outside and make a large snowball before chasing him through the expletive filled cabin. The shot lands and satisfyingly makes its way down his shirt. Revenge is sweet!

Our next stop is St. Johns, Newfoundland and we are quickly fueled and flying across the Atlantic to land at Bournemouth Airport in England. Bournemouth Airport was formerly called Hurn, the place where I flew my first flight in 1986. After landing the airliner here, I can't help feeling pleased with how this delivery is going now that we have made it to the halfway point. Les invites me to stay at his house and we enjoy some great home cooking before retiring to bed for a well-deserved sleep. After a good English breakfast in the morning, we are back in our seats again and heading out towards Turkey. The weather is perfect and the Boeing is flying very well. About one hundred miles from Turkey, I tune the standby radio to listen for the latest airport weather. I scribble it down for Les to read:

LTAC 1650z VRB/2kts 150m FZFG VV000 -5/-5 1020

This is bad news for us. There is only 150 meters (500 feet) of forward visibility and freezing fog at the airport. Even with the equipment we have available in this relatively modern jet airliner, the weather is below safe limits for us to shoot an approach to land. I scramble to find an alternate airport with better weather. Istanbul is a couple of hundred miles behind us and the weather is good there. Les agrees and I let air traffic control know our plan. They begin giving us headings to fly towards our diversion airport and after landing we are directed to a parking area for private aircraft. A set of stairs is placed next to the main cabin door and two smartly dressed representatives with clipboards greet us when I open the door. In contrast, Les and I are dressed in casual checked shirts and jeans. The surprised look on the faces of the agents is priceless. "Where are the pilots?" one of the agents asks. When they realize that we are the only two people on board, they simply cannot comprehend that pilots would dress this way. Les and I love to fly comfortably and so, under my own company rules, I don't expect my pilots to dress like Admirals of the Fleet!

Les and I chuckle at the situation and I explain to our shocked welcome party that the aircraft will still fly no matter how the pilots dress. One agent doesn't laugh and has a serious look of concern on his face. He tells us that airport security will never let us back onto the ramp while we are dressed in jeans. He says that if we leave the airport and exit the secure area, we will be stuck in Turkey unless we buy white shirts and shoulder bars to ensure we "look" like pilots! Les and I are looking forward to seeing a little bit of Turkey but we stubbornly play their game and ask for a place to stay in the airport tonight to avoid having to buy silly pilot shirts. The agent offers up the two leather couches in their office and that's where we stay.

I awake with the sun streaming through the office window and onto my face. My neck is sore from sleeping at an awkward angle on a hard leather cushion. Les and I are both keen to get into the air and we place the planning charts on a table to figure out the best route to Karachi. The door to the office unlocks and one of the agents who greeted us last night has arrived to start his shift. He has brought us pastries and wonderful thick Turkish coffee. I study the map with Les. Our diversion has inadvertently added almost five hundred miles to the last leg of our flight. This will really stretch the range of the thirsty Boeing but Les is comfortable with the route and so I file the flight plan. Our plan demands that we will get to our most fuel-efficient altitude of 37,000 feet without delay.

We taxi out and quickly get airborne, heading for Pakistan. The departure controller allows us to climb to 29,000 feet and we assume that this lower altitude must be a temporary stop for traffic above us. However, we stay at this altitude for quite some time. Soon, I question the controller and ask for a climb to our filed altitude of 37,000 feet. His response leads me to double check the flight plan paperwork and I quickly discover an error. The omission of a little "W" on the piece of paper confirms what the controller has stated. On a flight plan, the "W" tells air traffic controllers that we have the proper equipment needed to fly above 29,000 feet. I apologize for the error and confirm that we have suitable and working equipment to continue a climb but bureaucracy is in full swing. "Unable," comes the reply. Without the correctly filed flight plan in front of him, the controller is unwilling to accept a verbal confirmation for us to continue our climb. We will need to climb as soon as possible or we will not have the fuel to make it to Karachi. "Negative, unable." No matter how much I plead, the same answer keeps coming back. Then, the controller offers an olive branch. "Call the next controller early and maybe he can help you." I set to work recalculating the fuel burn numbers at 29,000 feet. I figure that we need to get above 34,000 feet to have any chance of making Pakistan without a fuel stop. I begin to look for another diversion airport.

I change frequency and call the controller. We have just entered Iranian airspace. I request a higher altitude and a more optimistic response follows, "standby." We stand by, and stand by and stand by some more. It isn't long before Les and I start to talk about a fuel stop in Tehran and the issue that the large American flag on the side of the old Boeing might cause. Relations between Iran and the United States are less than favorable and many American hostages are currently being held in prison there. I shiver at the prospect of landing in Iran. This time I am firm. "Sir, we must climb now or we will declare an emergency." A silence of several seconds seems to last several minutes but an answer eventually comes, "climb to flight level 350." The relief is immediate. Les asks for a celebratory coffee and I almost fall for it!

We finally touch down in Karachi on an extremely humid and dusty day. We probably have the least amount of fuel that this Boeing has ever had in the tanks but the new owners are thrilled with their new airliner and we are soon on our way to the hotel in the middle of town. The bustle of this city is exhilarating to me. Brightly colorod buses pass by with people hanging onto the outside window rails. Small mopeds weave precariously between speeding cars and everyone is constantly honking their horns for no apparent reason. I really like this place, it is so vibrant, colorful and alive. As always, I call Andrea as soon as I get to my room. My international calling card doesn't seem to work and so I make a quick direct call from the room phone. I keep the call very short. "I'm in Karachi, here's the number, call me back."

After freshening up, Les and I leave the hotel and go to a local market, where we are obvious targets for the sellers. There are so many stalls buried in the busy market and everything is held out in front of us: leather coats, pretty plates, carpets, hats, watches, radios and numerous pieces of jewelry. Some of the traders send their children to try and pull us toward their stands. Les buys a new leather jacket and after taking in some more sights of the city we decide to have dinner.

We are unsure about what to eat in Karachi and so decide on a more familiar dish. It is almost Chinese New Year and so we find a little Chinese restaurant close to the hotel. The food is great and the restaurant host is very courteous. We are relaxed and pleased with the delivery, despite the issues with weather and air traffic control. Between dishes, I ask the waiter for directions to the restroom. He clicks his fingers and a man comes to the table carrying a machine gun! He does not look at me. "Come with me," he says. I really don't know what do. The host comes over and nods his approval to me. I leave the restaurant, following the armed individual. We walk a few hundred yards down the street to a small shopping center. My guide sways the gun in front of him and scans the area ahead. I feel as if I have entered a war-zone and the bizarre actions surprise me. At the door to the shopping area he reaches into his pocket for keys, still scanning for "the enemy" whoever that might be. He unlocks the door, turns on the lights and we walk into a large corridor between the rows of closed shops towards a bathroom sign. It's not particularly comfortable to relieve myself with "Pakistan Rambo" waiting outside but I finish up and we return to the restaurant in a similar way to our outward journey. As I sit down at the table, Les stares at me with wide eyes waiting for my story. I shrug my shoulders and smile. "Do you need to go Les?" Unsurprisingly, he doesn't!

After a nice sleep, I wake early with a plan to absorb some more sights of the town, despite my strange experience last night. As I wait for a local bus to arrive, I notice some black charring on the ground close to the entrance near the hotel. I ask the doorman about it. "Terrorists," he says. He explains that a terrorist recently stopped there and detonated a car bomb. The blast killed the bomber and thirteen hotel guests who had boarded a bus parked next to the car. I am shocked. I have not heard about this tragic incident on the news. He points in the distance and tells me that there was another car bomb that detonated earlier this week, near the American consulate. It killed another twelve people and injured fifty others.

Suddenly, I realize why I was issued an armed guard to use the restroom last night. The doorman explains that many westerners have been kidnapped and murdered by terrorist organizations in Karachi. A chill shoots down my spine as I walk to the spot of the bus bombing with the doorman. He lists off details of several other deadly incidents that have taken place close to where we are standing. Despite this, he doesn't seem too concerned for my safety and urges me to enjoy exploring the city without fear. It is hard to do, especially when I arrive into the city center.

As I walk around, I notice that there are people on every street corner with guns on display. I hadn't seen this yesterday and it concerns me. I ask a local. He explains that former President of Pakistan, Benazir Bhutto, will be driving through the city today after her return from exile. In response, General Musharraf has released many political prisoners and so people are expecting trouble. This is enough for me. I get the distinct impression that the area around me is a "hair trigger" away from a gunfight. My initial desire to take a stroll through the city quickly changes to one of wanting to leave Karachi without delay. I go back to the hotel, book myself on a flight to Dubai and pack up my things.

In the hotel lobby, I return the key and ask to pay my bill. Something shocks me, it must be a mistake. It's the phone call I made to Andrea. They have charged me $600 for it! I explain that there must be a mistake. The call I made was for no more than one minute and I ask them to re-check. They do not seem to care and so I ask for the Manager. He doesn't seem too keen to correct this obvious mistake either. Something in their body language tells me that they have run this scam before. My politeness leaves and I become angry. I don't have time for this and I do not want to miss my flight. "I'll pay for my room and I will pay $20 for the phone call." I put enough cash down to cover this and begin to walk away. Immediately, some shouting starts and an armed guard near the front door lowers his gun and charges towards me. Am I back in Africa?

"I'm calling the police," I say in a raised voice and as if by magic a police officer walks into the lobby. It becomes obvious that he is in on the scam too. I have no choice if I am to catch my flight. I leave the hotel in a rage, $600 lighter. As the taxicab whisks me to the airport, I say nothing and stare out of the window. I feel sorry for the ordinary people of Karachi who are busy trying to feed their families and enjoy their lives while this corruption and terror exists around them. I meet Les at the airport as he is booked on the same flight. We settle into our seats and I peer out of the window as we taxi to the runway. I spot the Boeing 737 we delivered yesterday and I notice that the American flag has already been removed.

I am finishing my airline meal and I finally relax. As I drink a glass of red wine, I begin a conversation with myself. I have been ferrying for several years now. I never dreamed that I would be ferrying for so long but I'm thrilled that I have successfully delivered aircraft like the 737. I am very proud of my delivery record, I have seen so much of the world and I've met so many wonderful people. I have educated myself by exploring areas of the planet that I never read about in schoolbooks and I've seen so many varied cultures up close. But, the events in Karachi continue to play on my mind. The stress of managing my business and continuing with such a dangerous occupation is finally starting to get to me. Many ferry pilots are still perishing at a high rate. Alex just recently crashed in Goose Bay, killing her and her young daughter. It's a tragic waste and an event that really affects me. Alex had decided to push on in bad weather with a broken Cessna that would eventually fail her altogether. Nickki and the people in Goose Bay were waiting for her to arrive to celebrate her birthday; it was the reason she brought her daughter along but they never made it. I can see each fatal crash replay in my mind. I know the person, the plane and the area so well. My attitude has been changing recently and I have been approaching each aircraft as a potential coffin, waiting for my good fortune to run out. It is an extremely unhealthy and distressing way to start each flight. I have pushed my luck far too many times and I suspect that whatever I have remaining is close to running out. I will soon be getting married. Andrea has always known me as a ferry pilot but I rarely mention the true hazards I experience. I know that it is time for a change.

As we touch down in Dubai, I decide that I will begin to wind down my ferrying business and go back to pursuing my airline flying dream. As if by fate, I receive a call from "Diet Pepsi" John asking me to consider him for more deliveries. As we talk, John mentions a pilot position opening at his regional airline and I say I will consider it. I still have a few ferrying jobs to complete and so I catch my connection to fly onto my next delivery. I have so many things running through my mind but I know that the end of my ferrying career is in sight.

During one of our fuel stops in the old Boeing

BUSTED DUSTER

Ayres Thrush 660 Crop-duster
USA, Canada
(2,007nm 15.3 flying hours)

"It is late when the phone rings in my hotel room. Apparently, there is a lot of damage to my aircraft and so I get dressed and head back to the airport. The winds are gusting violently as we drive and snow is being blown from the tops of snow banks as tall as me. As I approach the large crop duster, my flashlight illuminates what is left of the ailerons. They are flapping around in the wind and the thick metal control lock in the cockpit is broken in half, snapped like a twig. My heart sinks. This is not going to be a quick fix. I help to push the battered aircraft into a nearby hangar and I call Joe."

It is two months since the 737 delivery: This crop-duster delivery is one of the most unusual types I have been asked to ferry. I can't resist. For me, saying no to something challenging like this is like walking away from a rollercoaster at the fairground; not knowing how fast the ride is, what the view at the top is like and how stomach wrenching the drop might be is a worse feeling than not riding at all. Joe's aircraft delivery business is thriving like mine. He too is employing delivery pilots to meet demand and he calls to ask if I have time to deliver a large crop-duster to Portugal. Before I can answer, he explains that it is not a normal aircraft. It is a purpose built, one of a kind, single seat duster with a very powerful turboprop

201

engine up front. It has a massive eight-hundred-gallon tank, or hopper as it's known, installed to store the chemicals needed to "dust" the crops. The tank has been temporarily converted to carry the fuel needed to fly across the Atlantic. It sounds like a beast of a machine and Joe knows that I can't say no. "You'll be on your own to figure out how to fly it," he says. That seals the deal for me.

The varied number of aircraft types I fly as a contract ferry pilot makes it almost impossible to maintain absolute familiarity on all but the most common aircraft. Like cars, each aircraft manufacturer has a slightly different placement of the throttle, the seat adjustment is different, the engine instruments have different displays and the location of switches varies between types. This demands a careful and methodical routine before flying each aircraft. First, I check the basic documents for legalities and then the logbooks to ensure the aircraft has been determined to be airworthy, had all its required checks completed and all mechanical issues have been cleared. I sit in the cockpit, adjust the pilots seat, open & close the aircraft door and find the most relevant items I need to get safely airborne. Experience forces me to locate the fuse for the electric trim. I had a "runaway" trim once and I never want that to happen again. I find the fire extinguisher, the fuel shutoff valve and test the full range of the flight control wheel or stick: full back, full forward, full left and full right. Next, I grab the Pilots Operating Handbook (POH), find a coffee machine and a place to be alone. I note speeds, placarded cautions, maximum altitudes, fuel quantities and basic notes on any unique equipment installed after manufacture. This process can take one or two hours before I feel ready to fly.

Luckily, there are very few different types of aircraft engines. Maintaining a thorough operational knowledge of engines makes jumping from one aircraft to another relatively easy. The dials may look different in the cockpit but the aim is always the same, keep the engine happy! Spending hour upon hour monitoring engine gauges and learning the "sweet" spot of each type allows quick identification of issues. Lycoming, Continental, Pratt & Whitney and Garrett – the seasoned ferry pilot has most of the operating parameters memorized. Getting airborne in unfamiliar types of aircraft takes an old fashioned smooth and steady approach. Each aircraft has its own unique personality and I'm cautious to respect the type and limit my initial control movements to ensure I am as smooth as possible. Some aircraft are stable, some are not, some are twitchy and others are like flying bricks! Occasionally, an aircraft is so unique that the only way to understand how it will fly is to jump in and fly it. As I walk across the ramp towards the crop-duster, I know that this will be one of those occasions.

I simply didn't appreciate just how large this "little" single engine crop-duster would be. It's thirty-six feet long, eleven feet high and it looks very impressive. A huge propeller dominates the front with a large exhaust pipe poking through the side of the engine cowling. Between the engine and cockpit is the huge hopper that Joe had told me about. I climb the four steps into the single-seat cockpit just behind the wing. I look out at the wingspan and realize just how large it is. At fifty-five feet, this is over half the wingspan of the Boeing 737 passenger airliner I just delivered. I go through my routine and find my way around the cockpit. This aircraft has a wonderful Pratt & Whitney PT6 turboprop engine up front. All I need is a starter switch, ignition switch, fuel control and an exhaust gas temperature gauge. I tell the factory representative that I will take the duster around the pattern, just to ensure everything works correctly before I set off. With a burst of flame, the engine comes to life.

The first issue arises as I begin to taxi out towards the runway. In these larger tail-wheel aircraft, the control stick must be held fully back to unlock the tail-wheel and allow a turn on the ground. No matter how hard I try, I cannot get the tail-wheel to unlock. I shut down and the mechanics come to investigate. After a little adjustment, I try again and it works well. The hopper is empty and so I only have 230 gallons of fuel in the wing tanks. This is enough for about two and a half hours of flying time with a small reserve. Once full, the hopper will add almost 5,000lbs of weight, extending my flying time to over eleven hours for the Atlantic crossing.

Without the extra weight of fuel on board, the 1,250hp engine accelerates the duster quickly. The torque of the propeller turns the aircraft sharply to the left requiring a quick boot load of right rudder to straighten it. I shove forward on the stick to raise the tail-wheel and before I know it I am airborne. So much for smooth and steady! My eyes are everywhere, inside and outside of the cockpit. I try to gauge which pitch attitude gives me the most comfortable climb rate as I massage the throttle lever to ensure the roaring engine stays cool. It is quite difficult to read the engine and airspeed gauges as the aircraft is shaking & vibrating like crazy. This aircraft is certainly not built for the comfort of the pilot! Once I gain a little altitude, I begin to figure out how much control input is needed to achieve smooth turns and climbs at varying airspeeds. The control forces required to keep the heavy machine steady are quite large and I know that this is going to be a tiring delivery. After ten minutes, I bring the duster around and land. I touch down on the two main wheels and then lower the tail-wheel back to the ground. I take the opportunity to try the reverse pitch thrust, which works surprisingly well. I accept the aircraft and top off the wing tanks. I also add three hundred gallons to the hopper for my first leg. Dusk is setting in as I climb towards the lights of Atlanta and north towards my first stop in Ohio.

It has been a long day and after almost 4 hours of flying I am feeling quite fatigued from the vibration and effort needed to fly the duster. My destination airport has a short runway and basic lights available for my landing. Nobody will be around when I land, which concerns me a little. I remember a friend in England who was flying an older tail-wheel "warbird" to a small private airfield one night. In the darkness, he misjudged the landing, bounced and flipped upside down. He was trapped in the cockpit, unable to free himself. A small fire began and spread quickly. His remains were found the next morning. I am thinking about this accident but continue into the night towards the small runway in an aircraft that I am still trying to figure out. I am not aware that fatigue is seriously affecting my decision-making abilities.

Before I land, I fly around the airport quite low to check that the runway is clear and to check the lighted windsock. The wind is relatively calm and the landing works out well. As I touch down, I feel so much relief that I relax the control forces and my tired mind. I have just committed a "cardinal sin" in a tail-wheel aircraft. The end of the runway comes up at me very quickly and I am not reacting.

My tail-wheel instructor's words come rushing back to me, "NEVER stop flying until you reach the hangar." I finally react as I heave the stick full back with maximum reverse and maximum brakes. I try to keep the duster straight to avoid a ground loop. I stop just before the last runway light with some new rubber laid at the end of the short runway. If I had floated just a few more yards, I would have ended up in a ditch. I am extremely mad at myself for continuing to fly in such a weary state. I am furious that I have let my tiredness distract me away from controlling an aircraft I am being paid to take care of. After I secure the duster, I get into my car and drive home, vowing never to put somebody's aircraft at risk like this again.

Andrea and recently moved close to the small airport in Ohio. It is nice to spend the evening at home before my delivery flight but I am back at the airport very early the next morning. The crop-duster towers over the small private aircraft parked alongside and quite a few people are checking out the unusual visitor. It takes a long time to fill almost 1,000 gallons of jet fuel and the airport Manager informs me that I have just doubled their quarterly jet fuel sales in one visit! I lay out my maps and double-check the weather. My plan is to fly from Ohio to Maine, where I will clear customs and get my export stamp. I will then fly to St. Johns, Newfoundland before heading to the mid-Atlantic stop of Santa Maria in the Azores. My last leg will be to the destination airport in Portugal. At the slow cruise speed and current fuel burn, I estimate that each leg will take around 5-6 hours. I am more aware of the effects of fatigue and so I will take it easy on this flight and choose to stay in Newfoundland before completing my Atlantic crossing. The weather looks good for the entire trip. In fact, there is a great wind window forecast across the Atlantic in a couple of days, which should make the crossing a little quicker.

As I begin loading up, I stumble across a problem. I have nowhere to put my Atlantic survival kit. I will wear my rubber suit as normal but there is simply no room in the small cockpit for the life raft, flares, locator beacon, first aid kit and the warm clothing I need for cold Newfoundland. I have no other choice; the raft, first aid kit and my clothes bag will have to go into the small lockable compartment in the back of the plane. If I need them, I will just have to figure out how to get them. I keep the other items with me in a little box under the pilot's seat, along with my empty apple juice container. My charts and flight log sit neatly on top of the instrument panel and I am ready to go. I don't have room for soup on this flight, which makes me sad.

As I lift off, I see my tire marks on the runway from the previous night. "Never again," I promise myself. With the extra fuel on board, the takeoff run is much longer than before, but the huge wings and the powerful engine lift me into the air just a few hundred feet down the runway. Flying in the daytime is far more pleasant but the ever-present shuddering still makes the flying challenging. The view from the small pod-like cockpit is great. Crop-dusting requires a pilot to fly extremely low and maneuver quickly to position for successive passes over a field of crops. With so many potential objects to hit, such as power lines, telephone wires and water towers, a good crop-dusting aircraft always has excellent all-round visibility for the pilot.

This visibility makes the seven-hundred-mile journey to Maine a very pleasurable trip. Most of the flat ground below me is lightly covered with snow but large irrigation circles are still visible. There is heavier snow packed onto the mountains around northern Pennsylvania and into Vermont as I fly on and gaze down. The views are stunning and this helps to make the journey pass quickly. I listen to the weather recording at Portland Airport. A strong and gusty crosswind is blowing. This will make the approach challenging. It is during this approach that I finally "click" with the wonderful duster. I feel as if I am connected to the controls and I am in complete control of every movement. The landing is pretty, despite the gusts and I feel quite satisfied as I taxi towards the customs office to complete the routine paperwork exchange and receive my red stamp of approval.

I am not on the ground for very long. I have one more 5-hour flight to complete before I will sleep. Leaving Portland, I fly almost parallel to the beautiful and rocky coast of Maine until reaching Nova Scotia. I cross a two hundred mile stretch of ocean before spotting the coastline of Newfoundland in the distance. My destination of St. Johns is located on the southeastern tip of this beautiful Atlantic island. The flight has gone very well and as night falls, the large runway comes into view. I make another satisfying landing. I am really growing to like this duster. I taxi and park near to a hangar that should offer some shelter from the evening elements. As soon as the engine stops, I grab the large metal control lock and attach it to the stick. This will prevent the controls from banging around in the wind. The ground crew helps me to tie down the wings and tail and I am happy to get to the warm Aeroshell FBO office.

Before too long, I am in an airport van and heading towards the largest town in Newfoundland for a beer and a good sleep. St.

Johns is the most easterly city in North America making it a perfect launching point for my Atlantic crossing. During the winter, it is guaranteed to be cold and windy here and tonight is no exception. I am happy to be in the warm hotel bar and bump into another ferry pilot, Richard, a fellow Brit. He has flown from Europe in a "V" tail Beech Bonanza like the one Graham owned. He is on his way to western Canada and is planning to leave early the next morning. We enjoy some good conversation as hundreds of fishing boats rock around in the harbor outside. I am very relaxed but as soon as I get to my room the phone rings. It is very bad news.

A few minutes later, I am in the van again and heading back to the airport. I am told that an airliner has been damaged by the same freak gust of wind that has damaged the duster. The tower controller estimates the main gust at well over 100 mph. I am dressed in many layers and a thick wool hat as I cross the icy ramp towards my aircraft. It is still tied down but there is a chilling noise coming from the ailerons. The wind is making them violently bang around up and down against the stops. I am mortified as I get closer and see the damage, which is incredible for such a short-lived gust of wind. The thick metal aileron control rod has been sheared in two and is sticking up into the air. The large aileron itself is banging around so hard that the metal skin has a concertina look to it. The most amazing damage is in the cockpit. The thick metal control lock has snapped, despite being designed to hold the flying controls in place for all of the strong winds this duster may encounter in its working life. I am glad that I was not in the air when this weather phenomenon hit. I beg the staff for a place in the hangar to try and limit any more damage. The hangar is packed but after moving several aircraft into new positions, we finally open a space large enough for the busted duster and we carefully push it inside.

I take photos of the damage for Joe, the owner and insurance company. There is nothing more I can do here and so I go back to the hotel to call Joe. He has already heard back from the people at the factory. They estimate that it will take several weeks to fix the duster. This ferry flight has come to an end, for now. I know that another commitment will prevent me from completing the delivery after repairs are made. I am proud of my "can-do" attitude when ferrying but this is one of those times when I simply can't do anything except head home. Joe doesn't know it yet, but I realize that this may well be my last ferry flight and I really hate to end it this way. I book an airline flight home. I consider catching a ride with Richard in the Bonanza but it is late and I don't want to wake him. I go back to the hotel, quite dejected.

I am glad that I didn't fly with Richard as he had an unusual ferry pilot incident the next day. About two hours from St. Johns, Richard had the "call of nature" resulting from an especially greasy breakfast. The traditional ferry pilot apple juice container would not help him this time! The situation demanded some ingenuity and so Richard placed his Atlantic crossing charts onto the pilot seat, positioned himself appropriately and relieved himself. He then rolled the waste into a ball and opened the small vent window to his left. He threw the paper out into the slipstream of the propeller, which immediately sent the contents racing towards the left-hand side of the "V" tail. The brown mess immediately froze, causing a little vibration that Richard felt through the control wheel. Not too long afterwards, Richard began experiencing engine problems and so looked for somewhere to land. Over Arctic Canada his options were a little limited but he spotted a small ice runway and headed for it. On the way down, he found a moment to chuckle, even though he knew he might slide off the runway and be killed. He pictured the rescuers arriving to find his mangled aircraft with a bunch of frozen feces on the tail. He wondered if they would classify the accident as a "turd strike!" Thankfully, Richard landed safely and made repairs before flying onto his destination several days later.

Since I began ferrying aircraft, I only failed to deliver two aircraft. One had mechanical issues and the other was this crop-duster. However, the commitment keeping me from completing the duster delivery is an opportunity to begin a new chapter of my flying career. One-week later, I am seated in a Regional Jet simulator in Denver, ready to begin my training. "Diet Pepsi" John from the ATP delivery is my new boss. I wrongly assume that my ferrying career has ended.

The large Ayres Thrush crop-duster during the delivery flight

Flying a Canadair Regional Jet for a US airline

PART THREE

REWARD

Moving Up

"You are already at your origin,
but you can always decide your destination."

FLUFFY SEAT

I am about to fly my thirteenth flight in a regional jet for the airline I have joined. Randy is finishing up my training and I expect to be signed off for line flying by the end of tonight. It is cold and windy as we taxi our jet towards the runway at Chicago O'Hare Airport. The ground controller is extremely busy and it takes a great deal of concentration to keep situational awareness as dozens of other aircraft taxi around us. The line of aircraft waiting to depart ahead of us is long and we sit for almost 40 minutes before we are finally cleared for takeoff.

I have flown twenty-three hours in the fifty seat Canadair Regional Jet and I am feeling quite comfortable. It is my turn to fly again and Randy hands over controls to me at the end of the runway. I push the two thrust levers forward and raise the nose to begin a climb into the night sky. Randy reaches over to raise the gear lever. Almost immediately a red warning light flashes and a loud computer generated voice sounds, "*Gear Disagree, Gear Disagree!*" There is an issue with our undercarriage. I continue to fly, trying my best to ignore the problem until we can get some altitude and ensure we keep clear of other departing aircraft. Chicago has some of the busiest airspace in the world and so it is several minutes before we are clear of the departure area and have the chance to tell air traffic control about our predicament. Randy gets the emergency checklist out. It appears that the wheels did not retract properly into the gear wells as we can hear the nose-gear in the wind beneath us. First, Randy tries to recycle the gear but the front wheel is jammed and won't retract. Randy calls the controller on the radio and declares an emergency.

It's not like the movies, there is no panic and no sweat is running from our brows. Randy is carefully and systematically working the problem using the checklist while I concentrate on navigation and flying. This type of task management is something my instructor emphasized during every simulator session of my two months of intense training. Randy has finished the emergency checklist so he calls our flight attendant Elizabeth on the inter-phone to explain the situation and asks her to prepare for an emergency landing. Then, he calls our company to inform them of the issue, allowing them ample time to set up a gate and an agent to help re-accommodate our passengers. Last, he makes a calm and professional announcement to the cabin to let our passengers know what to expect. He turns to me to ask how I am doing. I bring him up to-date with where we are, our current fuel state, current weight and the route air traffic is planning for our landing on the longest available runway. We will be landing in five minutes. I ask Randy for any advice or tips. "Just land smooth," he says!

It is a busy time for arrivals and departures at O'Hare but the airport is temporarily closed for our emergency landing. Randy and I expect the nose wheel to collapse on touchdown and so I plan to hold the weight off the nose until we are at a slow speed. As I turn to line up with the runway, I see dozens of red flashing lights either side. As we touch down, I gently hold back pressure on the control wheel to keep the nose-wheel in the air just a few inches above the tarmac. As I carefully lower the jammed wheel I anticipate a collapse but the gear stays put. I hear the passengers applauding in the cabin behind us. As we come to a stop, Randy resumes control and tries to steer the CRJ off the runway but he has no steering control. We quickly realize the problem. The steering torque links must have disconnected during our takeoff roll. Randy suspects that the ramp crew did not connect them properly after we were pushed back from the gate earlier this evening. We sit on the runway and wait for a tug to pull us back to the gate. After we are safely at the gate, Randy explains the issue to the passengers and they follow us to another aircraft to try again. It is very late when we finally land in Lansing, Michigan. Randy thanks the passengers for their patience and then announces to them that he has just signed me off as the newest First Officer at our airline. Many of the passengers shake my hand and offer their congratulations as they leave the aircraft. I can hardly contain my beaming smile. I have three silver stripes on my shoulder and I am an airline pilot.

The next morning, Randy lets me fly the last leg back to Chicago. As I land for the first time as a qualified First Officer, I think back to the long journey I made to reach this moment. I think of the barriers that tried to stop me and the inspiration I drew from others to keep going. I have earned my stripes and I am glad I kept going. I think about ferry pilots that started with the same airline dream but never got to sit here. Some gave up, and many are dead. As I sit in my furry covered seat in the cockpit of this regional jet, I feel a world away from the mouse infested room back in Southampton. Perhaps this was always my destiny? Certainly, determination and a great deal of luck have helped but whatever it was, the feeling of satisfaction and pride is as wonderful as I ever thought it would be.

SWEAT BOX

I have been airline flying for the past few years. The CRJ is a little cramped for our passengers but the cockpit has become a comfortable and familiar office for me. My routes are varied but usually consist of flights up and down the eastern United States. I have deviated around a countless number of thunderstorms and I have de-iced the little jet hundreds of times during several seasons of regional flying. About two years ago, I was selected to join the Training Department and I am now a busy simulator instructor. Today is a special day because the FAA has just approved my examiner status after watching me administer a successful simulator check flight for Stefano. I am now authorized to issue type ratings and airline transport certificates to new CRJ captains. This is the highest instructor certificate I can attain and I am incredibly proud to be trusted with the responsibility.

On paper, I am a designated representative of the FAA. My examiner life is dictated by thick manuals and lots of forms. I realize that I have become a part of the bureaucracy that stalled my own career but I make sure to keep a healthy dose of common sense with me in my new position. Pinned to the wall in front of my desk is a reminder from Douglas Bader, "the rules are written for the obedience of fools and the guidance of wise men." When I am not training, I still maintain my flying currency with the airline. The only difference is that I now fly as the captain. My first captain training flight was an interesting experience.

I am flying the approach into Bangor, Maine in the CRJ but it is the first time I am flying in the captain's seat. The cockpit is incredibly familiar but moving three feet to the left of my normal seat feels weird. I am used to flying with my right hand and using my left hand to work the thrust levers but now I must change this around. I know Bangor Airport very well. This is where I had many aircraft tanked before setting off across the Atlantic. The Archer with the broken wing was tanked here. This is where Simon talked to me about the dangers of ferry flying before he was killed in Greenland. This was the customs stop on my first ever Atlantic ferry flight to America in a small twin-engine Piper Aztec. And now, I am about to land on the same runway for the first time as an airline captain.

The touchdown is smooth and I taxi towards the terminal close to the ferry tanking shop. There is a small Piper Arrow outside, tanked up and ready to leave. I can see the ferry pilots' rubber survival suit on the wing. I wonder if he brought soup? I am keen to see if the ferry pilot is somebody I know but I do not see him. As I shut down our two General Electric CF34 engines at the gate, I receive my weather pack for the return leg back to Washington DC. I get a little distracted and start to look at the Atlantic weather instead. I guess the route this ferry pilot might be flying as the weather looks awful across the Atlantic today. I begin to draw possible routes he might choose to avoid the icing areas, and the altitudes he might choose for the best tailwinds. My instructor, Jason, asks what I'm doing. "Oh, nothing," I say. I finish my required paperwork and make a regular "sit back and relax" passenger announcement. I try not to become too distracted as I taxi by the little Arrow one more time on my way to the runway. This time, I see the ferry pilot but I do not recognize him. I wave, wishing him luck with my gesture. He waves back.

Thirty minutes later, we are in the cruise at 30,000 feet. The flight is going well, the ride is smooth and all systems are working well. I go back and use the restroom and look at myself in the small mirror on the wall as I wash my hands. I am wearing four silver stripes on my shoulders. I still cannot believe that I am an airline captain. Just a few years ago, I was the guy in the rubber survival suit preparing to fly another oceanic crossing, not knowing if it would be my last flight. I have been extremely lucky, I know that now. I vow to enjoy every flying day that I am given as I freshen up, return to my fluffy, finish my coffee and prepare for the next landing.

I never believe that I will be ferry flying again.

TYPHOON RACE

Citation Jet CJ1
USA, Russia, Japan
(6,023nm 28.1 flying hours)

"I issue an ultimatum to the Japanese man. Either we leave now or we will get caught in the path of a monster typhoon. I stand by the door of the 6-seat Citation business jet and motion my reluctant passenger inside. Infuriatingly, he stops to make another phone call. I begin to close the door but he finally gets in before it is shut. I rush the pre-takeoff checks, something I hate to do. If I have any chance of beating the deadly storm I will need to get airborne immediately."

My ferrying career has long since finished but I am keeping a promise I made to a Japanese broker I worked with several years ago. We had such a good business relationship that I offered them unlimited ferrying advice, even after I stopped ferrying myself. I am quite surprised to hear from them because I was quite embarrassed by the last delivery I managed for them. A few years back, they asked me to deliver a small Citation private jet. At the time, I was unable to leave the United States as my immigration papers for my work permit was being processed. Instead, I employed another pilot to take my place and help with the delivery. This was a huge mistake as he grossly overspent on fuel, flights and the hotel budget. Even worse, he delivered the customers aircraft with damage to the areas around the fuel caps and wings due to his careless "manhandling" during fueling. To add insult to injury, his final bill to me contained thousands of dollars of extras I simply could not verify. I paid up but vowed never to employ him again. I lost around $10,000 on this delivery but wrote-off the loss against "you win some, you lose some." I felt terrible for the aircraft owner and I couldn't stop apologizing to the broker. I was truly shocked to receive a check from my Japanese contact the following week to help cover my loss. The respect I have for the Japanese and their business integrity was solidified by this incredibly kind action.

It seems that the broker is truly struggling to find a suitable ferry pilot for a Cessna CJ1 corporate jet and the delivery is very important to them. I have no options to offer and so I decide to repay their past generosity by dusting off my ferrying equipment one last time. I check my schedule and get approval from my airline to fly the hours I will need to deliver the jet. I will be on a tight timetable as I only have five days to complete the delivery before I need to be back to flying the CRJ. To be safe, legal and rested, I will need to catch a flight home in just under four days. My ferry pilot friend Curt is willing to help so that I can speed up the delivery process and make it a little more fun. My flight back to America leaves Japan in 90 hours. This will be a race against the clock. I look at my watch.

90 hours to go. I have just landed in Wichita, Kansas, the home of Cessna Aircraft. Curt is on his way and so I fall back into my old ferrying routine and begin preparing the paperwork allowing me to accept delivery of the CJ1. It's a very sleek looking aircraft, with a "T" tail and two small jet engines at the back. Inside is quite luxurious with lots of leather and fancy polished wood fixtures. I check the mini-bar, it is full. This will help speed up our transit in

Russia. The cockpit has the latest flight management system and glass displayed instruments. This is a very nice corporate jet and I begin the cockpit checks to ensure all the equipment is working properly. The TCAS (Traffic Collision Avoidance System) is not working and so a mechanic says he will look at it. I don't want him to rush the repair but I ask him to be as quick as possible.

84 hours to go. Curt has just turned up. He has brought several cans of New England Clam Chowder soup with him. Old habits die-hard and we will both eat like ferry pilot kings on this flight! Unfortunately, the TCAS system is still not fixed. Every hour that passes is less time available to be able to complete the delivery. The maintenance person estimates another hour to fix the unit. If there are any more delays during the delivery I will have to leave and return to work before getting to Japan. The maintenance guy brings bad news. The TCAS unit will have to be replaced. A new unit is on its way from somewhere close by. I insist that we must be airborne by 8pm, otherwise the 5,000-mile flight to Japan will have to be postponed. I re-plan the route while I wait. There will be no time for sight-seeing on this trip and the line on my map is as straight as I can plan. The first stop will be Grant County Airport in southeastern Washington state. It is a 4-hour flight in the CJ1.

79 hours to go. We are level at 42,000 feet, much higher than the bigger CRJ I fly for the airline can fly. I record every engine parameter accurately to set our "normal" benchmark for the delivery flight. The small jet flies wonderfully. The controls are light and responsive and there is plenty of power with just Curt and I on board. Unfortunately, the black of night is our view out of the front. Fortunately, there is not much of a headwind and so we are making good progress. I have calculated a Cinderella inspired "pumpkin" time at each stop. This is the latest time we must leave to ensure that I will make my flight back to Chicago from Tokyo. I check my watch often.

75 hours to go. We have just landed at Grant County. The "pumpkin" time is one hour from now, so we quickly fuel up and get back into the air. I check my progress sheet. We are ahead of schedule by twenty minutes. I relax a little and start reviewing the charts for our next airport, Fairchild Airport in northern Washington.

73 hours to go. I wish that it was not so dark outside. The gorgeous Olympic Mountains are around here but all I see is black. The approach chart shows that we will be paralleling the mountain range as we descend towards the runway. We will not see the peaks as the local airport weather shows a low cloud base of 500ft above the runway. I concentrate hard to fly an accurate approach, but the winds are whipping us around quite badly. I am struggling to maintain the centerline of the runway and we are being slowly pushed towards the mountains. The airspeed is particularly hard to control and I'm rapidly changing the thrust, reacting to each gust as it hits us. I get that "feeling", one of being uncomfortable and not in control. It's a horrible sensation of knowing you are just along for the ride. Decision time: I put on full power and pull the nose back. Curt raises the flaps and wheels as I climb to a safe altitude to recompose myself. I check our fuel load and we have plenty. I decide to try the approach again and it's much better the second time around. The touchdown isn't pretty but I am happy to be on the runway. I am tired and Curt is tired. I think back to the duster flight and decide we will stop for the night. I will re-plan our delivery tomorrow morning to make up the time.

65 hours to go. We are awake, refreshed and ready to leave. I calculate that we can afford to make one more sleep stop before landing in Japan. We will push through until we reach Russia today. It is clear this morning and we can see the amazing jagged mountains that were hidden last night. Snow is covering the tops and they look particularly spectacular. This is the northern coast of America in Port Angeles. Canada is just twenty miles across the Strait of Juan de Fuca. Our next leg will be to the Alaskan airport of Valdez. We will clear customs there. I call the flight service briefer and get a weather synopsis and a review of NOTAMs affecting our flight. These "Notices to Airman" are issued by the FAA to communicate navigational beacon outages, chart changes and relevant airport notices. We depart and make a turn to climb over beautiful Vancouver Island as the sun rises. I can see the snow-covered Rockies in the distance, a sight that becomes even more impressive as we fly towards the growing mountain range stretching out beneath us. I look down and stare at every crevice passing below, wondering if any human feet have ever touched these remote areas. I'd hate to have an emergency here. I think back to my flight in the Cirrus as I prepared to crash into those snowy Canadian mountains. I am glad that I am sitting at 40,000 feet in a jet today.

61 hours to go. The weather is atrocious as we descend towards the fishing town of Valdez. The only approach available is a basic non-precision approach without too much radar assistance. It demands a lot of concentration as the terrain surrounding the airport rises from sea level to 12,000 feet. The approach is constructed to keep us over an inlet as we descend. It is very like the approach into

229

Narsarsuaq Greenland, which allows the descent to take place between the mountains and over the fjord. There is a point on the approach beyond which we do not have the power to out-climb the mountains ahead. The decision to land must be made almost five miles before reaching the airport to ensure an adequate safety margin. The visibility is reported right at five miles and so the decision to land or not will be made right at the last minute. We are almost at the decision point but we are still being bounced around in the clouds. I am ready to push the power up and climb away when Curt says, "got it, runway ahead!" I have a quick peek through the windscreen. I can barely see the runway and so I go back to flying the approach using the instruments. We are now committed to land. At three miles, I look up again and see the black runway ahead with bright white runway markings. As we reach a half mile from the runway, the rain is pounding down on us. Something catches my eye on the end of the runway but I can't figure out what it is. Then I realize what I am looking at, there are white "X" markings on the end of the runway meaning that the runway is closed. "Shit," I say out loud. The weather briefer didn't tell us about a closed runway but I have no other choice except continue. There is nowhere else to go. I scan up and down the runway for any other obstacles and aim my touchdown just past the wooden white "X" marker. We land safely and taxi off.

56 hours to go. "How is our new runway?" I am worried that we are in trouble but the guy behind the desk chuckles and is apologizing to us. He explains that the runway is officially open but he had trouble getting into work and didn't have time to remove the wooden markers. My adrenaline is still pumping but I take a very

230

deep breath! Curt is checking the Citation for any damage and thankfully it is fine. I hand the paperwork pack to the customs official and take a break before our next leg. Soon enough, we are airborne again. Curt is flying the next couple of legs and so I head back into the comfortable leather seats for a snooze. Our next stop is Adak Island at the end of the Aleutian chain.

52 hours to go. Curt calls me up front to give me the bad news. The cloud base at Adak is below legal minimums and so he has sensibly decided to divert to Dillingham Airport just ahead of us. I take my seat next to Curt and help him by getting the approach charts for Dillingham and tuning in the radio to listen for the latest airfield weather. The cloud base in Dillingham is 600 feet above the runway and we need 500 feet to be able to shoot the localizer approach to runway 19. It's barely legal and it will be another difficult approach to fly. Curt does a great job and we soon pop out of the cloud to see the long runway straight ahead. I look at my watch. Each delay is decreasing my chances of making the flight in Japan.

49 hours to go. On the ground, we talk to a weather briefer. He says that the Adak weather is improving and so we fill the tanks of the CJ1 with fuel and set off again. As promised, the familiar runway at Adak is soon in view below the clouds. I remember back to that quick refuel we had to perform in the King Air with Mr. Nakamura and Mr. Yamashita. It was ridiculously windy then and there is no change today. I chuckle as I remember the events of that fun King Air flight. It seems that no ferry flight is ever destined to go as planned. After fueling, our next leg will cross the International Date Line, the line of zero degrees of longitude that vertically splits the earth into two. I think back to crossing the Equator, the horizontal zero-degree latitude line with Graham in the Cirrus as we flew to South Africa. I really can say that my ferrying career has allowed me to crisscross the world!

39 hours to go. We have just flown past the spectacular volcanoes on the Kamchatka Peninsula in Russia. I stare through the glass of my office window and see a myriad of colors associated with the setting sun. A perfectly flat layer of clouds is below us, absorbing the colors. The peaks of three huge smoking volcanoes are visible poking through the tops of the clouds and they cast a breathtaking shadow over the red and orange blanket below. It is a breathtaking sight. Curt touches down smoothly on Russian soil before we are met by Valery, who receives his bounty of miniatures. It's just like old days! We are both exhausted and ready for some sleep. Valery arranges a taxi to take us to our hotel. The hotel is ten miles from the airport, on the outskirts of Petropavlovsk. The taxi driver does not speak English and we soon wish we knew the Russian word for "slow down!" This guy is driving like a maniac on dark potholed streets. We see headlights in the distance heading straight for us, as he weaves away at the very last moment. We are terrified and shout at the driver to stop but he doesn't. The lunatic taxi driver makes a call on a huge mobile phone while steering with one hand. I cannot understand what he is saying but it seems like he is arguing with somebody. We hit the side of a parked car before he reluctantly listens to our shouting and stops the car within walking distance of the hotel. I don't give him a tip. Annoyed, he takes a swig of vodka and screeches off.

29 hours to go. It is bright and sunny outside my hotel room when I wake. The room is about half the size of a cheap motel room

232

in America but its twice as expensive. The wallpaper is a mix of brown and orange straight from the 1970s. Despite this, the small bed is quite comfortable and I slept well. The next morning, I head downstairs to meet up with Curt and have breakfast. Curt is chuckling at a sign on the wall in the lobby:

"Dear guests! We are welcoming you in our hospitable house. Hotel was built in 1973 according to personnel project. Hotel has good access road and payable car park.

Having knowing the hotel regulation and our peninsula special features help you in an extreme situation. In case of earthquake, do not panic, keep calmness and self-control. Earthquake up to force 5 is not dangerous. If earthquake is more strong do the following – Take safest place at room. Stand aside from glass. After shocks finished you have 30 seconds for evacuation from hotel. THANK YOU for the choice of hotel."

We allow ourselves thirty minutes to explore the town a little and to walk off our breakfast. The whole area around the hotel is pretty run down but there are people dotted everywhere. Most are just standing around with their hands in the pockets of large overcoats. Everyone looks suspicious. It is a busy town but nobody seems to be talking. The bustle of movement is the only noise we can hear. I get a real sense and feel of old Russia, which is wonderful despite the lack of eye contact from the locals. We turn a corner and see a Soviet tank on display. It is dark green and is marked 111, a memorial to the victims of the Crimea War. Further down the street is a large statue of Lenin watching over the two western visitors looking up. We are soon back at the airport, ready to fly our longest leg.

20 hours to go. I am flying the approach to Sendai Airport on the eastern coast of Japan. We have been flying for almost five hours, which is near the maximum endurance of the CJ1. During the flight, I studied the weather charts. There is a typhoon rapidly moving towards southern Japan and close to our destination. The typhoon will hit tomorrow morning and so I have already decided we will continue on and finish the delivery tonight. The CJ1 needs to be safely inside a hangar before the sun rises.

16 hours to go. We have cleared customs in Sendai and I have completed the mountain of paperwork necessary to import the aircraft. Curt and I are ready to leave for our destination near Okayama, three hours flying time away. The broker has sent a representative to meet us in Sendai. He is a very nice man and says he has booked a hotel for us in the center of Sendai. I apologize and tell him we must continue flying tonight. "Perhaps you reconsider, nice rest, nice sushi?" It's a lovely offer but I explain our predicament. He doesn't seem to understand. "We must leave now, right now," I say as clearly as I can. "Hhhmm, maybe you fly tomorrow afternoon?" I don't have time to discuss this or argue as I know that our destination airport closes after sunset and more debating is only going to cause us more issues. "No, we are leaving now, with or without you." I feel bad for him but I know this is the right decision.

12 hours to go. We can see the edge of the typhoon to the south as we make our approach to land in Kohnan. The tower controller has stayed on duty to switch on the runway lights for us.

The cost for this is $750! After landing on the short runway, I help to put the Jet into its new hangar. I can't stop looking at my watch. There is a bullet train leaving from Okayama in two hours and I want to be on it. We have some paperwork to complete before I can go. While I wait for some more paperwork to arrive, I begin to look at a book about the Boeing 747. It is written in Japanese and so I can't understand a word, but it fascinates me. We go back to the hangar and walk through the aircraft to check for any damage or broken items. Everything is good and the delivery is completed with lots of smiling faces surrounding us. As Curt and I get into a taxi cab, somebody hands me a wrapped package, which I put into my bag and we drive off. This taxi journey is so different from the one in Russia. The driver is wearing white leather gloves and the cab is immaculate. He drives on the correct side of the road, at the correct speed and correctly keeps his eyes on the road!

8 hours to go. Curt is staying in Japan a little longer and so I board the sleek bullet train to Tokyo without him. The rail journey takes just under four hours and snakes through some amazing countryside, rolling hills and the stunning temple city of Kyoto. I see none of it as I am asleep for the entire journey.

2 hours to go. I have just checked-in for the flight to Chicago. As I approach the gate, I see the aircraft being prepared for my flight back home, it's a beautiful Boeing 747. As I take my seat on-board and the cabin door closes I remember the package that I was handed in Kohnan. I open it up and smile when I realize that it's the Japanese 747 book I saw on the shelf in the office!

My last ferry flight is finally complete.

I have survived.

I recline my seat and fall asleep.

I will be back in my office tomorrow.

The Citation CJ1 in Russia with a TU-154 in the background

With Sir Richard Branson in the cockpit of an Airbus A320

EPILOGUE

It is now more than thirty years since I flew my first flight in the DeHavilland Chipmunk and almost fifteen since my last ferry flight in the CJ1. Today, I am an Airbus Captain flying for a major airline in the United States. Appropriately, the route I fly the most often is the Pacific Ocean crossing between San Francisco and the Hawaiian Islands. My unlikely schoolboy dream came true.

Before each of my flights today and with the swish of my pen, I assume total responsibility for a $100 million aircraft, five crew members and almost two hundred passengers. Each person on-board entrusts their safety to me completely, but few will realize that I continue to draw on the experiences I gained while flying those small aircraft around the world to ensure I make the right decisions. I no longer fly in a yellow rubber suit and I do not eat lukewarm soup, but there are many more similarities than differences between airline flying today and my ferry flying past. I still approach each flight with the same attitude that served me so well back then. The safety of the aircraft and of those on-board are my absolute primary concern and so I maintain a suspicious eye when thumbing through the maintenance logbook history before I depart. Once airborne, I ensure I have a thorough plan, I keep a watchful eye on changing weather patterns, I always have an "escape" planned and I maintain a check of my progress using a flight log, just as I did when I was ferrying.

Safety is the biggest improvement I have seen since I started flying and the numbers are staggering. Back in 1950, some 80,000 passengers would take to the sky in 1,200 aircraft every day. When I takeoff in my Airbus, I join over 8,000,000 passengers in 100,000 aircraft! But despite the massive increase in airline travel over the years the risk of a fatal crash has plummeted. In 1950, thirteen out of every one million flights would end with a fatal crash. Today, just 0.2 flights would result in a fatality and that number continues to fall. Sadly, during my time as a ferry pilot I was aware of six fatal crashes involving a delivery pilot, far higher than these averages. Other colleagues have perished since I stopped ferrying and each loss continues to cause me much sadness. The numbers do not lie; professional ferry flying is still one of the most dangerous jobs in aviation and I'll never forget any of the pilots whose destination was tragically altered by fate.

For this book, I selected what I believed to be some of my more interesting or unusual ferry flights to write about, but there are several that I didn't mention:

- My first Atlantic crossing was made from east to west in a Piper Aztec with fellow pilot Brendan. Ashley and Lesley flew next to us in a second Aztec from England to Florida. The weather cooperated and allowed a relatively uneventful crossing. With the benefit of experience as hindsight, I know that luck was a major factor keeping us safe during this crossing. The ferry tanks from those Aztecs were sold to a ramp worker in Gander who used them as makeshift moonshine stills!

- The coldest I have ever been in an aircraft was during a winter delivery flight in a Britten Norman Islander with my friend Mark. The heater quit as we left Iceland but the fuse to reset it was in the nose compartment, meaning we couldn't get to it until we landed in Greenland several hours later! This aircraft became a medical evacuation aircraft. Sadly, a few years later the aircraft would crash in Canada, killing the pilot.

- One of my several weather diversions led me to meet John and his wife Sandra in Ireland. John was an Air Canada Captain who heard and spoke to many Atlantic ferry pilots on the radio throughout his career. However, I was the first one he had met in person, which led to a wonderful night at the local pub, talking to relatives of Charles Lindberg and enjoying a very comfortable sleep in their lovely house.

- A Piper Arrow delivery from Canada to England was extra enjoyable when the bubbly owner Mike decided to come along. I ended up buying a thermometer from a café freezer to keep an eye on the outside air temperature, which allowed us to safely cross the Greenland ice-cap. A few years later, this aircraft suffered an engine failure after takeoff requiring Mike to ditch into the ocean. He was rescued by a fishing vessel but the Piper Arrow was lost at sea.

After spending several years flying the CRJ, my airline career led me to work for Sir Richard Branson, the person I used as an inspiration when designing my first ferrying website. On a sunny day in April 2011, I was privileged to be in the cockpit for a very historic flight. Richard and pioneering Apollo astronaut Buzz Aldrin were in the cabin along with many other dignitaries as we flew our A320 low over San Francisco. We were joined on our left wing by the first ever private spaceship, VSS Enterprise. It was an incredible sight that I will never forget. Tragically, in 2014 a test flight malfunction destroyed VSS Enterprise, killing pilot Michael Alsbury who was one of the pilots flying with us that day. Aviation safety continues to improve because of the lessons learned from accidents like this and because of the sacrifices that pilots like Michael continue to make.

At the time of writing, Joe is still ferrying aircraft. He is one of the most experienced delivery pilots in the world and is in great demand. Graham from the South Africa story has retired from ferry flying and "turd strike" Richard is now an airline captain in Singapore. "Diet Pepsi" John has left the aviation industry and currently works in the medical field. Les got a taste for ferrying after our Boeing 737 delivery to Pakistan and started his own ferrying business. Eugene "Hideaway" Bridges is an extremely successful live musician who tours the world with his band. He was recently honored with the Albert King Lifetime Award for outstanding contributions to traditional blues music. My air-race friend Peter Hunter wrote many wonderful flying books and inspired me to write this book. Peter died before I could finish writing but he left me one of his flying watches, which I wear often when I fly. Bill Goldfinch finally saw an exact replica of his Colditz glider successfully fly before he passed away.

Unfortunately, the Grumman (G-OMOG) that I flew on my first solo was destroyed in a landing accident but the DeHavilland Chipmunk (WD373) that I first flew on that day in 1986 at Hurn

Airport is currently part of the flying collection at the Imperial War Museum in Duxford, England. I chose WD373 as the license plate for my car.

There are several inspirational people who helped to guide me on my journey but who are not included in these stories. Without the friendship of Tony Sheppard, the wisdom of Rob Hirst, the guidance of David Scouller and the generosity of Louisa Dickson my dream would have forever stayed a dream. I very much appreciate Julius Frank, Dave Everhart, Matt Graber, my wife and several others for reading and correcting my many attempts at storytelling while assembling the various chapters of this book and for their encouragement to continue writing.

As for the bureaucrats, the JAA in Europe eventually amended their regulations to include language addressing the common laser eye procedure. Even the Royal Air Force is considering relaxing their rules as the US Air Force already allows their flight crews to correct vision with laser surgery. Unexpectedly and unsolicited, I received an unrestricted medical from the JAA four years after I had first applied for it in Ireland. It is currently sitting in a drawer at home.

Andrea and I are happily married and live in California. Rob came out of the "security bushes" to be my best man and Joe took time away from ferrying to stand beside me as a groomsman. There were several ferry pilots in our wedding party, including Torben from Cirrus ferrying days and Les from the Boeing story. A few years after I stopped ferry flying, Andrea obtained her pilots license. We currently own a Grumman Cheetah, the same type that I flew at Eastleigh for my first solo flight. I have kept my promise to Larry and

I take people up for fun flights as often as I can. I intend to continue this until I am no longer able to fly myself. Our Grumman is kept at a small airfield where Richard at SkyView Aviation still installs fuel tanks for aircraft being ferried across the Pacific, as he did for me so many years ago. My interest is always raised whenever I see a ferry pilot preparing for a crossing. I watch them pull on their rubber suit and I wonder if they have any cans of cold soup in their bags.

My Dad was diagnosed with a rare string of Alzheimer's Disease several years back. Thankfully, his memory loss has been gradual but it was the overwhelming reason for writing down these stories. If I should ever end up losing my memory, I intend to make myself some lukewarm soup and read this book to remind myself of my past life! What will I think about this crazy journey?

Standing next to VSS Enterprise after a publicity formation flight

With Andrea, flying our Grumman Cheetah around California

Thank You

Keith & Gillian Askham, Curt Arnspiger, Group Captain Sir Douglas Bader, Michael Barrong, Larry & Jean Bax, Paul Beaver, Captain Rob Bendall, Andrew Berry, Sir Richard Branson, Captain John Brennan, Eugene 'Hideaway' Bridges, Andrew Bruce, Ashley Buckle, Jim Carney, Richard & Alice Connell, David Cooke, John Cook, Captain Simon Cook, Captain Simon Cottrell, Justin Cox, Captain David Curtles, John Davies, Valery Daydov, Louisa Dickson, Dustin Dryden, Jim Douse, Squadron Leader Neville Duke, Dave Everhart, Richard Evans, Paul Fahie, Christine Farrell, Captain Jim Fox, Julius & Deanna Frank, Captain John Gijsen, Captain Matt Graber, Mike Glinternick, Flight Lieutenant Bill Goldfinch, Linda Green, Costas Hadjiefthymiades, Ronan Harvey, Noel Hayes, Pam Heather, Martin Hill, Captain Rob Hirst, Tim & Kathy Hodgkins, Captain Les Hounsome, Richard Hunt, Peter & Celia Hunter, Flight Lieutenant Ernie Jones, Hardy Kalitzki, Captain Mike Keifer, Captain Torben Kiese, Candice Larson, Captain Joseph Leone, Alain Lutz, Paul Marsh, Lesley & Mervyn Maynard, Adrian McCabe, Mark McClelland, Captain Richard McGready, Richard McGuire, Paul McQuillan, Steven Middendorp, Captain Jason Morford, Lieutenant Commander David Morgan, Keith Morton, Andy Morris, Johnny Moss, Ralph Mullers, Phil Mummery, Ranald Munro, Robin Musham, Minoru Nakamura, Rob Oade, Bob O'Neill, Denise Osborne, Captain Scott Orozco, Richard & Conchita Ortenheim, Ben Parker, Captain Lance Pamperin, Shaun Patrick, Stefano Pensa, Matthew Perry, Lisa Ponting, Captain Tyfingur Porsteinsson, Nickki Powell, Captain Paul Preidecker, Brian Preston, Mark Pringle, Geoff Prout, Andre Quinton, Caroline Rabson, Kathy Ridguard, Geoff Rosenbloom, Lasse Rungholm, Nick Russell, David Sawdon, Group Captain David Scouller, Ian Seager, Tony Sheppard, Dave Shepperd, Martin Smith, Captain Randy Smothers, David Stapleton, Franz Strohmann, Joe Thorne, Graham Tickton, Piet VanBlerk, Brendan Walsh, Alan Williams, Captain Kim Willis, David Wilson, Sarah Wilson, Toshimitsu Yamashita and Eguchi Yukifumi.